Strangers at Our Door

Strangers at Our Door

Zygmunt Bauman

polity

The right of Zygmunt Bauman to be identified as Author of this Work has been asserted in accordance with the UK Copyright, Designs and Patents Act 1988.

First published in 2016 by Polity Press

Polity Press
65 Bridge Street
Cambridge CB2 1UR, UK

Polity Press
350 Main Street
Malden, MA 02148, USA

ISBN-13: 978-1-5095-1216-4
ISBN-13: 978-1-5095-1217-1 (pb)

A catalogue record for this book is available from the British Library.

Library of Congress Cataloging-in-Publication Data

Names: Bauman, Zygmunt, 1925- author.
Title: Strangers at our door / Zygmunt Bauman.
Description: 1 | Malden, MA : Polity, 2016. | Includes bibliographical references.
Identifiers: LCCN 2016002256 (print) | LCCN 2016009972 (ebook) | ISBN 9781509512164 (hardback) | ISBN 9781509512171 (paperback) | ISBN 9781509512195 (Mobi) | ISBN 9781509512201 (Epub)
Subjects: LCSH: Emigration and immigration--Social aspects. | Immigrants--Public opinion. | Refugees--Public opinion. | BISAC: SOCIAL SCIENCE / Sociology / General.
Classification: LCC JV6225 .B396 2016 (print) | LCC JV6225 (ebook) | DDC 304.8--dc23
LC record available at http://lccn.loc.gov/2016002256

Typeset in 12.5 on 15 pt Adobe Garamond by
Servis Filmsetting Ltd, Stockport, Cheshire
Printed and bound in Great Britain by CPI Group (UK) Ltd, Croydon

For further information on Polity, visit our website:
politybooks.com

Contents

1 Migration Panic and its (Mis)uses

TV news, newspaper headlines, political speeches and Internet tweets, used to deliver foci and outlets for public anxieties and fears, are currently overflowing with references to the 'migration crisis' – ostensibly overwhelming Europe and portending the collapse and demise of the way of life we know, practise and cherish. That crisis is at present a sort of politically correct codename for the current phase of the perpetual battle waged by opinion makers for the conquest and subordination of human minds and feelings. The impact of the news broadcast from that battlefield now comes close to causing a veritable 'moral panic' (by the commonly accepted definition of that phenomenon, as recorded by the English Wikipedia, the concept of 'moral panic' stands for 'a feeling of fear spread among a large number of people that some evil threatens the well-being of society').

As I write these words, another tragedy – one born of callous unconcern and moral blindness – lies in wait to strike. Signs are piling up that public opinion, in cahoots with the ratings-covetous media, is gradually yet relentlessly approaching the point of 'refugee tragedy fatigue'. Drowned children, hastily erected walls, barbed-wire fences, overcrowded concentration camps and governments vying with each other to add the insult of treating the migrants as hot potatoes to the injuries of exile, narrow escape and the nerve-racking perils of the voyage to safety – all such moral outrages are ever less news and ever more seldom 'in the news'. Alas, the fate of shocks is to turn into the dull routine of normality – and of moral panics to spend them-selves and vanish from view and from consciences wrapped in the veil of oblivion. Who remem-bers now the Afghan refugees seeking asylum in Australia, hurling themselves against the barbed-wire fences of Woomera or confined to the large detention camps built by the Australian govern-ment on Nauru and Christmas Island 'to prevent them from entering its territorial waters'? Or the dozens of Sudanese exiles killed by the police in the centre of Cairo 'after having been deprived of their rights by the UN High Commission for Refugees'?[1]

Massive migration is by no means a novel phenomenon; it accompanied the modern era from its very beginning (though time and again modifying, and occasionally reversing, its direction) – as our 'modern way of life' includes the production of 'redundant people' (*locally* 'inutile' – excessive and unemployable – due to economic progress, or *locally* intolerable – rejected as a result of unrest, conflicts and strife caused by social/political transformations and subsequent power struggles). On top of that, however, we currently bear the consequences of the profound, and seemingly prospectless, destabilization of the Middle-Eastern area in the aftermath of the miscalculated, foolishly myopic and admittedly abortive policies and military ventures of Western powers.

And so the factors behind the present mass movements at the points of departure are twofold; but so also are their impact at the points of arrival and the reactions of the receiving countries. In the 'developed' parts of the globe in which both economic migrants and refugees seek shelter, business interests covet and welcome the influx of cheap labour and profit-promising skills (as Dominic Casciani pithily summed it up: 'British employers have become savvy at how to get cheap foreign workers – with employment agencies working hard on the continent to iden-tify and sign up foreign labour'[2]); for the bulk of the population, already haunted by the existential frailty and precariousness of their social standing and prospects, that influx signals, however, yet more competition on the labour market, deeper uncertainty and falling chances of improvement: a politically explosive state of mind – with politi-cians veering awkwardly between incompatible desires to gratify their capital-holding masters and to placate the fears of their electors.

All in all, as things stand now and promise to be standing for a long time to come, mass migra-tion is unlikely to grind to a halt; neither for the lack of prompting nor for the rising ingenuity of attempts to stop it. As Robert Winder wittily remarked in the preface to the second edition of his book, 'We can park our chair on the beach as often as we please, and cry at the oncoming waves, but the tide will not listen, nor the sea retreat.'³ The building of walls in order to stop migrants short of 'our own backyards' comes ridiculously close to the story of the ancient philosopher Diogenes rolling the barrel in which he lived to and fro along the streets of his native Sinope. Asked the reasons for his strange behaviour, he answered that, seeing his neighbours were busy barricading their doors and sharpening their swords, he wished also to add his own contribution to the defence of the city against being conquered by the approaching troops of Alexander of Macedonia.

What has happened most recently, however, in the last few years, is an enormous leap in the numbers added by refugees and asylum seekers to the total volume of migrants knocking at Europe's doors; that leap has been caused by the rising number of 'falling', or rather already fallen, states, or – to all intents and purposes – stateless and so also lawless territories, stages of interminable tribal and sectarian wars, mass murders and catch-as-catch-can, round-the-clock banditry. To a large extent, this is the collateral damage done by the fatally misjudged, ill-starred and calamitous military expeditions to Afghanistan and Iraq, which ended in the replacing of dictatorial regimes by the open-all-hours theatre of unruliness and the frenzy of violence – aided and abetted by the global arms trade unleashed from control and beefed up by the profit-greedy arms industry, with the tacit (though all too often proudly displayed in public at international arms fairs) support of GNP-rise-greedy governments. The flood of refugees pushed by the rule of arbitrary violence to abandon their homes and cherished possessions, of people seeking shelter from the killing fields, topped the steady flow of the so-called 'economic migrants', pulled by the all-too-human wish to move from barren soil to where the grass is green: from impoverished lands of no prospects, to dreamlands rich in opportunities. Of that steady stream of people seeking the chance for a decent life standard (a stream flowing steadily since the beginning of humanity, and only accelerated by the modern industry of redundant people and wasted lives[4]), Paul Collier has the following to say:

> The first fact is that the income gap between poor countries and rich ones is grotesquely wide and the global growth process will leave it wide for

several decades. The second is that migration will not significantly narrow this gap because the feedback mechanisms are too weak. The third is that as migration continues, the diasporas will continue to accumulate for some decades. Thus, the income gap will persist, while the facilitator for migration will increase. The implication is that migration from poor countries to rich is set to accelerate. For the foreseeable future, international migration will not reach equilibrium: we have been observing the beginnings of disequilibrium of epic proportions.[5]

Between 1960 and 2000, as Collier calculated (having available at the time of his writing only the statistics up to 2000), 'what took off, from under 20 million to over 60 million, was migration from poor countries to rich ones. Further, the increase accelerated decade by decade . . . It is a reasonable presumption that 2000 continued this acceleration.' Left to its own logic and momentum, we may say, the populations of poor and rich countries would behave like the liquid in corresponding vessels. The number of immigrants is bound to rise towards equilibrating, until the levels of well-being even up in both 'developed' and 'developing (?)' sectors of the globalized planet. Such a result will in all probability, however, take many decades to reach – even barring the unanticipated turns of historical fate.

Refugees from the bestiality of wars and despotisms or the savagery of famished and prospectless existence have knocked on other people's doors since the beginnings of modern times. For people behind those doors, they were always – as they are now – strangers. Strangers tend to cause anxiety precisely because of being 'strange' – and so, fearsomely unpredictable, unlike the people with whom we interact daily and from whom we believe we know what to expect; for all we know, the massive influx of strangers might have destroyed the things we cherished – and intend to maim or wipe out our consolingly familiar way of life. Those people with whom we are used to cohabiting in our neighbourhoods, on city streets or in work places, we divide ordinarily into either friends or enemies, welcome or merely tolerated; but to whatever category we assign them, we know well how to behave towards them and how to conduct our interactions. Of strangers, however, we know much too little to be able to read properly their gambits and compose our fitting responses – to guess what their intentions might be and what they will do next. And the ignorance of how to go on, how to deal with a situation not of our making and not under our control, is a major cause of anxiety and fear.

These are, we might say, universal and extemporal problems when there are 'strangers in our midst' – appearing at all times and haunting all sectors of the population with more or less similar intensity and to a more or less similar degree. Densely populated urban areas inevitably generate the contradictory impulses of 'mixophilia' (attraction to variegated, heteronymous surroundings auguring unknown and unexplored experiences, and for that reason promising the pleasures of adventure and discovery) and 'mixophobia' (fear of the unmanageable volume of the unknown, untamable, off-putting and uncontrollable). The first propulsion is city life's main attraction – the second being, on the contrary, its most awesome bane, especially in the eyes of the less fortunate and resourceful, who – unlike the rich and privileged, capable of buying into 'gated communities' to insulate themselves from the discomforting, perplexing and, time and again, terrifying turmoil and brouhaha of crowded city streets – lack the capacity to cut themselves off from the numberless traps and ambushes scattered all over the heterogeneous, and all too often unfriendly, distrustful and hostile, urban environment, to whose hidden dangers they are doomed to remain exposed for life. As Alberto Nardelli reports in the 11 December 2015 issue of the *Guardian*, 'Nearly 40% of Europeans cite immigration as the issue of most concern facing the EU – more than any other issue. Only a year ago, less than 25% of people said the same. One in two of the British public mention immigration as among the most important issues facing the country.'[6]

In our increasingly deregulated, multi-centred, out-of-joint world, this permanent ambivalence of urban life is not, however, the only thing that makes us feel uneasy and afraid at the sight of homeless newcomers, that arouses enmity towards them, that invites violence – and also the use, misuse or abuse of the migrants' all too visible destitute, woeful and powerless plight. We can identify two extra elements that do so, triggered by the peculiar traits of our post-deregulation mode of life and cohabitation – two factors apparently quite distinct from each other, and so predominantly affecting different categories of people. Each of the two factors intensifies the

resentment and pugnacity towards immigrants –
but in different sectors of the native population.

The first impulse follows, even if in a somewhat
updated form, the pattern sketched already in
Aesop's ancient tale of the Hares and the Frogs.[7]
The Hares of that tale were so persecuted by the
other beasts that they did not know where to go.
As soon as they saw even a single animal approach
them, off they used to run. One day they saw a
troop of wild Horses stampeding about, and in
quite a panic all the Hares scuttled off to a lake
hard by, determined to drown themselves rather
than live in such a continual state of fear. But just
as they got near the bank of the lake, a troop of
Frogs, frightened in their turn by the approach of
the Hares, scuttled off and jumped into the water.
'Truly', said one of the Hares, 'things are not as
bad as they seem'. No need to choose death over
life in fear. The moral of Aesop's tale is straightforward: the satisfaction that this Hare felt – a
welcome respite from the routine despondency of
daily persecution – he has drawn from the revela-
tion that there is always someone in a yet worse
pickle than he himself.

Hares 'persecuted by the other beasts', and
finding themselves in a plight similar to that

suffered by those in Aesop's tale, are plentiful in our society of human animals – in recent decades, their numbers have kept growing, and seemingly unstoppably. They live in misery, debasement and ignominy amid a society set to out-cast them while boasting the glory of its unprecedented comfort and opulence; having been routinely derided, reproached and cen-sured by those 'other human beasts', our 'Hares' feel offended and oppressed by being demeaned and denied worthiness by other people, at the same time as berated, ridiculed and humiliated by the court of their own conscience for their all-too-evident impotence in levelling up with those above them. In a world in which everyone is presumed, expected and prompted to 'be for himself (or herself)', such human Hares, refused respect, care and recognition by other humans, are, just like Aesop's 'Hares persecuted by other beasts', cast into that 'hindmost' that has been written off as the legitimate Devil's spoil – and kept there for the duration, with no hope, let alone a trustworthy promise, of redemption or escape.

For the out-casts who suspect they have reached the bottom, the discovery of another bottom beneath that to which they themselves have been pushed is a soul-saving event, redeeming their human dignity and salvaging whatever is left of their self-esteem. The arrival of a mass of homeless migrants stripped of human rights, not only in practice but also by the letter of the law, creates a (rare) chance of such an event. This goes a long way to explaining the coincidence of the recent mass immigration with the rising fortunes of xenophobia, racism and the chauvinistic variety of nationalism – and the astonishing as much as unprecedented electoral successes of xenophobic, racist, chauvinistic parties and movements and their jingoistic leaders.

The Front National, led by Marine Le Pen, gathers votes mostly among the bottom layers – disinherited, discriminated against, impoverished and fearing exclusion – of French society, mustering their support with the explicitly stated or tacitly presumed rallying call 'France for the Frenchmen'.[8] From people threatened with practical, even if not (thus far) formal, exclusion from their society, such a call can hardly be ignored: after all, nationalism provides them with the dreamt-of life-boat (a resurrection device?) for their fading or already defunct self-esteem. What saved the 'white trash' of the Southern States of the US from the extremes of an excruciating, suicidal self-hatred was the presence of subhuman negroes denied even the one privilege they were entitled – at least in their own minds – to boast of: their white skin. Being a Frenchman (or a Frenchwoman) is one feature (the only one feasible?) that puts their French counterparts in the same category as the good and noble, high and mighty people at the top, while sumultaneously setting them above the similarly miserable aliens, the stateless newcomers. Migrants stand for that sought-after bottom located even farther down – beneath the bottom to which the indigenous *misérables* have been consigned and committed; a bottom that may render one's own lot a little bit less than absolutely demeaning, and so a little bit less bitter, unendurable and intolerable. Migrants must be told they are, and kept, living on borrowed time – for the Frenchmen and Frenchwomen to at least, for better or worse, feel *chez soi*.

And there is one more exceptional (that is, reaching beyond the 'normal', extemporal distrust of strangers) reason to be resentful of the massive inflow of refugees and asylum seekers, a reason appealing mostly to a different sector of society – to the emergent 'precariat': to people afraid of losing their cherished and enviable achievements, possessions and social standing, rather than those human equivalents of Aesop's Hares, sunk in despair fed by having already lost them or never having been given a chance to attain them.

One cannot help but notice that the massive and sudden appearance of strangers on our streets neither has been caused by *us* nor is under *our* control. No one consulted us; no one asked our agreement. No wonder that the successive tides of fresh immigrants are resented as (to recall Bertolt Brecht) 'harbingers of bad news'. They are embodiments of the collapse of order (whatever we consider to be an 'order': a state of affairs in which the relations between causes and effects are stable, and thus graspable and predictable, allowing those within it to know how to proceed), of an order that has lost its binding force. Immigrants are an updated – 'new and improved', as well as more seriously treated – edition of those 'sandwich men' of the frivolously and rashly raving 1920s, carrying through the city streets jammed with gullible revellers announcements that 'the end of the world as we know it is nigh'. They, in Jonathan Rutherford's poignant expression, 'transport the bad news from a far corner of the world onto our doorsteps'.[9] They make us aware, and keep reminding us, of what we would dearly like to forget or better still to wish away: of some global, distant, occasionally heard about but mostly unseen, intangible, obscure, mysterious and not easy to imagine forces, powerful enough to interfere also with our lives while neglecting and ignoring our own preferences. The 'collateral victims' of those forces tend to be, by some vitiated logic, perceived as those forces' avant-garde troops – now setting up garrisons in our midst. Those nomads – not by choice but by the verdict of a heartless fate – remind us, irritatingly, infuriatingly and horrifyingly, of the (incurable?) vulnerability of our own position and of the endemic fragility of our hard-won well-being.

It is a human – all-too-human – habit to blame and punish the messengers for the hateful contents of the message they carry – in this case, from those baffling, inscrutable, frightening and rightly resented global forces which we (with sound reason) suspect of bearing responsibility for the agonizing and humiliating sense of existential uncertainty which wrecks and grinds down our confidence as well as playing havoc with our ambitions, dreams and life plans. And while we can do next to nothing to bridle the elusive and faraway forces of globalization, we can at least divert the anger they caused us and go on causing, and unload our wrath, vicariously, on their products, close to hand and within reach. This won't, of course, reach anywhere near the roots of the trouble, but might relieve, at least for a time, the humiliation of our helplessness and our incapacity to resist the disabling precariousness of our own place in the world.

That twisted logic, the mindset it generates and the emotions it lets loose provide highly fertile and nourishing meadows tempting many a political vote-gatherer to graze on them. This is a chance that a growing number of politicians would be loath to miss. Capitalizing on the anxiety caused by the influx of strangers – who, it is feared, will push down further the wages and salaries that already refuse to grow, and lengthen yet more the already abominably long queues of people lining up (to no effect) for the stubbornly scarce jobs – is a temptation which very few politicians already in office, or aspiring to an office, would be able to resist.

Strategies that politicians deploy to embrace that opportunity can be – and are – many and different, but one thing needs to be clear: the policy of mutual separation and keeping one's distance, building walls instead of bridges, and settling for sound-insulated 'echo-chambers' instead of hot lines for undistorted communication (and, all in all, washing one's hands and manifesting one's indifference in the disguise of tolerance) lead nowhere but onto the wasteland of mutual mistrust, estrangement and aggravation. Deceptively comfort-bringing (by chasing the challenge out of sight) in the short run, such suicidal policies store up explosives for future detonation. And so one conclusion needs to be equally clear: the sole way out of the present discomforts and future woes leads through rejecting the treacherous temptations of separation; instead of refusing to face up to the realities of the 'one planet, one humanity' challenges of our times, washing our hands and fencing ourselves off from the annoying differences, dissimilarities and self-imposed estrangements, we must seek occasions to come into a close and increasingly intimate contact with them – hopefully resulting in a *fusion* of horizons, instead of their induced and contrived, yet self-exacerbating, *fission*.

Yes, I am fully aware that choosing this course is not a recipe for a cloudless, trouble-free life and effortlessness in the task that demands our attention. It portends instead dauntingly lengthy, jolty and thorny times ahead. It is not likely to bring an instant relief to anxiety – it may even trigger, initially, yet more fears, and further exacerbate the extant suspicions and animosities. All the same, I don't believe there is an alternative, more comfortable and less risky, shortcut solution to the problem. Humanity is in crisis – and there is no exit from that crisis other than solidarity of humans. The first obstacle on the road to the exit from mutual alienation is the refusal of dialogue: the silence born of – while simultaneously bolstering – self-alienation, aloofness, inattention, disregard and, all in all, indifference. Instead of being seen as the dyad of love and hate, the dialectic of border drawing needs to be thought, therefore, in terms of the triad of love, hate, and indifference or neglect.

The situation in which we find ourselves at the threshold of 2016 is – incurably at the moment

– ambivalent, and theorizing its straightforward-
ness and un-ambiguity seems – if we attempt to
put it into practice – to store more risks than the
ailment it is pretending to cure. It won't accept
shortcut solutions, and if such solutions are
contemplated, this theorizing can't be put into
practice without exposing the planet, our joint/
shared domicile, to long-term menaces even
more catastrophic than our current joint/shared
predicament; whatever choices are resorted to,
what we need to keep in mind is that they can't
but affect our joint/shared (hopefully long)
future, and for this reason need to be guided by
the precept of reducing such dangers, instead of
magnifying them. Mutual indifference obviously
wouldn't pass the test.

I'll return to this issue in chapter 4, in which
Kant's recommendation – more than two centuries old, yet ever more topical – will be recalled,
deliberated and updated.

Let me for this moment remind you of another
message, coming from Pope Francis – in my
view, one of the very few public figures to alert us
to the dangers of following Pontius Pilate's ges-
ture by washing our hands of the consequences
of the current trials and tribulations, of which we

are all, simultaneously, to one degree or another, victims and culprits. On the vice or sin of indifference, Pope Francis had the following to say on 8 July 2013 during his visit to Lampedusa – when and where the current 'moral panic' and the ensuing moral débâcle started:

> How many of us, myself included, have lost our bearings; we are no longer attentive to the world in which we live; we don't care; we don't protect what God created for everyone, and we end up unable even to care for one another! And when humanity as a whole loses its bearings, it results in tragedies like the one we have witnessed . . . The question has to be asked: Who is responsible for the blood of these brothers and sisters of ours? Nobody! That is our answer: It isn't me; I don't have anything to do with it; it must be someone else, but certainly not me . . . Today no one in our world feels responsible; we have lost a sense of responsibility for our brothers and sisters . . . The culture of comfort, which makes us think only of ourselves, makes us insensitive to the cries of other people, makes us live in soap bubbles which, however lovely, are insubstantial; they offer a fleeting and empty illusion which results in indifference

to others; indeed, it even leads to the globalization of indifference. In this globalized world, we have fallen into globalized indifference. We have become used to the suffering of others: it doesn't affect me; it doesn't concern me; it's none of my business!

Pope Francis calls on us 'to remove the part of Herod that lurks in our hearts; let us ask the Lord for the grace to weep over our indifference, to weep over the cruelty of our world, of our own hearts, and of all those who in anonymity make social and economic decisions which open the door to tragic situations like this'. Having said that, he asks: 'Has anyone wept? Today has anyone wept in our world?'

2 Floating Insecurity in Search of an Anchor

The Shorter Oxford English Dictionary defines 'security' as a 'condition of being protected from or not exposed to danger' – but, at the same time, as 'something which makes safe; a protection, guard, defence': this makes it one of those not common (yet not uncommon, either) terms that presume/hint/suggest/imply an organic – and so once and for all fixed and sealed – elective affinity linking the condition to the assumed means of attaining it (a sort of unity akin to that which, for instance, is suggested by the term 'nobility'). The *condition* to which this particular term refers is highly and deeply, as well as unquestionably, appreciated and yearned for by most language users; the approbation and regard bestowed on it by the public rubs off thereby on its acknowledged *guards* or *providers*, to which its name also, in one fell swoop, refers. The means bask in the glory of the condition and so share in its undisputed desirability. Once this has been accomplished, a fully predictable pattern of conduct tends to be followed automatically, in the way typical of all conditioned reflexes. Do you feel insecure? Demand and press for more public security services to guard you, and/or buy more security gadgets believed to avert dangers. Or: do the people who elected you to high office complain of feeling insufficiently secure? Hire/ appoint more security guards and allow them also more liberty to act as they consider necessary – however unappetizing or downright loathsome and revolting the actions they might choose turn out to be – and advertise widely what you've done.

A heretofore unknown term – and one still unrecorded in dictionaries available in bookshops – 'securitization' has appeared quite recently in public speech, coined and quickly adopted in the vocabulary of politicians and media people. What this neologism is meant to grasp and denote is the ever more frequent reclassification of something previously thought

of as belonging to some other phenomenal category, as an instance of 'insecurity'; recasting
followed well-nigh automatically by transfer-
ring that something to the domain, charge and
supervision of security organs. Not being, of
course, the *cause* of such automatism, the above-
mentioned semantic ambiguity no doubt makes
its practising easier. Conditioned reflexes can do
without lengthy argument and laborious persua-
sion: the authority of Heidegger's 'das Man' or
Sartre's 'l'on' ('this is how things are done, aren't
they?') renders them so obvious and self-evident
as to be practically unnoticeable and unavailable
for questioning. A conditioned reflex itself stays,
safely, unreflected upon – at a safe distance from
the searchlights of logic. This is why politicians
gladly resort to the term's ambiguity: making
their task easier and assuring their actions a
priori of popular approval – even if not of the
promised effects – it helps politicians to con-
vince their constituencies that they are taking
their grievances seriously and acting promptly
on the mandate those grievances have been presumed to bestow.

Just one example, picked up at random from
among the most recent headline news: as the

Huffington Post reported shortly after the night of terrorist outrages in Paris:

> French President François Hollande said a state of emergency would be declared across France and national borders shut following a spate of attacks in Paris on Friday evening . . . 'It is horrifying', Hollande said in a brief statement on television, adding that a cabinet meeting had been called. 'A state of emergency will be declared', he said. 'The second measure will be the closure of national borders', he added. 'We must ensure that no one comes in to commit any act whatsoever, and at the same time make sure that those who have committed these crimes should be arrested if they try to leave the country.'[1]

The *Financial Times* reported the same presidential reaction under a no-beating-about-the-bush title 'Hollande's Post-Paris Power Grab': 'President François Hollande declared the national emergency immediately after the Nov. 13 attacks. It allows police to break down doors and search houses without a warrant, break up assemblies and meetings, and impose curfews. The order also clears the way for military troops to be deployed to French streets.'[2] The sight of broken-down doors, of swarms of uniformed policemen breaking up meetings and entering homes without asking for their residents' agreement, of soldiers patrolling the street in broad daylight – all these and similar scenes make a powerful impression as demonstrations of the government's resolution to go the whole hog, down to 'the heart of the trouble', and to allay or altogether disperse the pains of insecurity tormenting their subjects.

Demonstration of a firm intention and the resolve to follow it is (to use Robert Merton's memorable conceptual distinction) the 'manifest' function of those scenes. Their 'latent' function, however, is quite the opposite: to promote and smooth out the process of 'securitizing' the multitude of people's economic and social headaches and worries born of the ambience of insecurity – generated in turn by the frailty and fissiparousness of the current existential condition. The above-mentioned sights are after all guaranteed to create the atmosphere of a state of emergency, of an enemy at the gate, of plots and conspiracies – in sum, of the country, and so also of our own homes, facing a mortal danger. They are bound to entrench those 'up there' firmly in the role of the (sole, irreplaceable?) providential shield preventing awesome catastrophes from being visited on both.

Whether the manifest function of those sights has been successfully performed is, to say the least, a moot question. That they acquit themselves brilliantly of their latent function is not, however, open to doubt. The effects of the head of state flexing his muscle (and that of the security organs he commands) in public were as fast coming as they were in excess of all previous attainments by the current holder of the presidential office, until then found by opinion polls to be the least popular president in France since 1945. A fortnight or so later, Natalie Ilsley could sum up those effects under a title that leaves nothing to the imagination: 'After Paris, Hollande's Popularity Soars to Highest Level in Three Years':

One poll revealed on Tuesday an 'unprecedented' 20-point rise in the president's confidence rating to 35 percent in December – a level not seen since December 2012. According to French daily newspaper *Le Figaro*, results by polling agency TNS Sofres show that 35 percent of French people say they trust Hollande to deal with the aftermath of the attacks claimed by the Islamic State militant group (ISIS), an increase from 13 percent polled in August . . . Another poll published on Tuesday by Ifop-Fiducial for French weekly *Paris Match* and Sue Radio also showed a dramatic increase in support for Hollande. Based on the views of 983 French citizens, Hollande's approval rating soared from 28 percent in November to 50 percent in December.[3]

The widespread sense of existential insecurity is a hard fact: a genuine bane of our society that prides itself, through the lips of its political leaders, on the progressive deregulation of labour markets and 'flexibilization' of work, and thus, as a result, is notorious for propagating a growing fragility of social positions and instability of socially recognized indentities – as well as for unstoppable expansion of the ranks of the precariat (a novel social category, defined by Guy Standing primarily by the quicksands on which they are forced to move). Contrary to many an opinion, this insecurity is not just a product of politicians pursuing electoral gains, or of media profiting from panic-mongering broadcasts;

it is, however, true that the real, all-too-real, insecurity built into the existential condition of ever-widening sections of the population is welcome grist to the politicians' mill. That frailty is in the process of being converted into a major – perhaps even paramount – stuff of which the present-day technique of governing is fashioned.

Governments are not interested in allaying their citizens' anxieties. They are interested instead in beefing up the anxiety arising from the future's uncertainty and the constant and ubiquitous sense of insecurity – providing that the roots of that insecurity can be anchored in places which provide ample photo opportunities for ministers flexing their muscles, while hiding from sight rulers overwhelmed by the task with which they are too weak to cope. 'Securitization' is a conjurer's trick, calculated to be just that; it consists in shifting anxiety from problems that governments are incapable of handling (or are not keen on trying to handle) to problems that governments can be seen – daily and on thousands of screens – to be eagerly and (sometimes) successfully tackling. Among the first kind of problems there are such principal factors of the human condition as the availability of quality jobs, reliability and stability of social standing, effective protection against social degradation, and immunity from a denial of dignity – all those determinants of safety and well-being that governments, once promising full employment and comprehensive social security, are nowadays incapable of pledging, let alone delivering. Among the second, the fight against terrorists conspiring against ordinary folks' bodily safety and their cherished possessions easily grasps and holds fast the first fiddle – all the more so because of its chance of feeding and sustaining the legitimation of power and the effects of vote-collecting efforts for a long time to come; after all, the ultimate victory in that fight remains a distant (and thoroughly doubtful) prospect.

The Prime Minister of Hungary Viktor Orbán's laconic and tremendously catchy dictum 'all terrorists are migrants' provides the sought-after key to the government's effective struggle for survival – all the more so thanks to the implicitly smuggled suggestion of the symmetry of the link and a reciprocity of causation, and so a roughly complete overlap between the two thus-linked categories. Such an interpretation defies logic – but faith does not need logic to convert, brainwash and enslave minds; on the contrary, it gains in its holding power as it loses in its logical credentials. To the ears of governments wishing to redeem, against all odds, their seriously lopsided and steadily sinking *raison d'être*, it must sound like the horn of a salvage-boat sailing out from the dense, impenetrable fog in which the horizon of their survival struggle has been enveloped.

To the author of that dictum, the gains were immediate, while the outlays of putting money where Orban's mouth was were all but limited to a 4-metre-high fence along the 176-kilometre border with Serbia. When Hungarian respondents were asked in the December Median-HVG poll what comes into their minds when they hear the word 'fear', more people (23 per cent) named terrorism than cited illness, crime or poverty. Their overall sense of security had fallen considerably:

The respondents also had to indicate their feelings on a number of statements and mark the intensity of these feelings on a scale of 0–100. For example, 'immigrants pose health risks for the native population' (77), 'immigrants substantially increase the danger of terrorist attacks' (77), 'those who illegally

cross the borders will have to serve a jail sentence'
(69). The statement that 'immigration might have
a beneficial effect on Hungary because it would
remedy the demographic problems and would add
to the labor force' elicited little enthusiasm (24).[4]

Expectedly, Orbán's fence proved enormously
popular. If, in September, 68 per cent of the population approved of it, three months later '87%
of the population stand behind Viktor Orbán's
solution to the migrant problem' – and so by
proxy, let's make it clear, to the haunting spectre
of insecurity. As Roger Cohen, the *New York
Times* op-ed columnist, put it (in a different context) concisely: 'big lies produce big fears that
produce big yearnings for big strongmen'.[5]

We may hazard a guess that, if coupled with a
focus on a specific, visible and tangible adversary,
intensification of fear is somewhat more endur-
able than in the case of dispersed, scattered and
floating fears of unknown origin. It may even
prove to be, perversely, a satisfactory sort of
experience: once we decide that there is a task to
perform and that we are up to performing it, we
willy-nilly acquire a vested interest in the grandiosity of what we are about to perform and so, by

proxy, in the power of resistance we are likely to encounter. The more commanding and indomitable our task appears, the prouder and more flattered we are likely to feel; the more powerful and scheming the enemy appears, the higher the heroic status of those who dare to declare war on him. It is no coincidence that an absolute majority of Hungarian respondents approved of the statement 'Certain unnamed outside moving forces are behind the mass migration.'

Calling the nation to arms against an *appointed* (as Carl Schmitt proposed in his *Political Theology*) enemy gives an added advantage to politicians in frantic search of voters: such a call is bound to rouse the nation's self-esteem, and thereby earn the caller the nation's gratitude – at least, the gratitude of the (growing, or afraid of growing) part of the nation particularly strongly hurt and anguished by damage done to their standing in society and the fogginess of their life prospects, all threatening an imminent withdrawal of public recognition and so also of self-respect: a part yearning, for that reason, for some compensation (even if it is of an inferior value because of its generic, instead of personal, character) for their loss of personal status and dignity.

Finally, the policy of 'securitization' helps to stifle in advance our – the bystanders' – pangs of conscience at the sight of its suffering targets; it leads to the 'adiaphorization' of the migrant issue (that is, exempting them and what is done to them from moral evaluation). Once they have been cast in public opinion in the category of would-be terrorists, migrants find themselves beyond the realm of, and off limits to, moral responsibility – and, above all, outside the space of compassion and of the impulse to care. Indeed, if drilled by the policy of 'securitization', many people feel – knowingly or not – glad to be relieved of responsibility for the fate of the wretched, as well as of the pressures of a moral duty that otherwise would inevitably follow to torment the bystanders. For that relief – knowingly or not – many people are grateful. To whom? Obviously, to the muscle-flexing and tough-talking politicians.

As Christopher Catrambone observed in the *Guardian*:

Following the terror attacks in Paris and political scaremongering that followed, we have started putting these people at risk again. The human tragedy of people fleeing by sea to escape terrorism is being diminished by vitriolic accusations, the building of walls, and a fear that these refugees are coming to kill us. Most are just escaping war in the Middle East. But even when trapped between European anger and the violence that drove them out of their country, refugees still brave the worsening seas.[6]

Catrambone is not a panic-monger; being a member of Moas (the Migrant Offshore Aid Station), he knows the fate of people on the receiving side of 'securitization' better than most of us. According to the statistics compiled by his charitable search-and-rescue organization, 'the drowning of men, women and children fleeing war, poverty and oppression at sea remains a daily occurrence: since August 2014 Moas has rescued almost 12,000 people from the water'. Catrambone alerts and appeals:

The EU is predicting that 3 million refugees and migrants will have reached its territory by 2017. This will have a positive impact that will stimulate the economy. Ultimately that is why people are coming, will continue to come and cannot be stopped from coming to Europe. They seek the same thing we all want: something better. The reality is that these people will contribute to, not take away from, our economy. Yes, it will be rough in the beginning, but they are becoming part of Europe's future, whether we like it or not.

One more comment is in order. On top of being morally callous and odious, and socially blind as well as to a large extent groundless and often intentionally misleading, 'securitization' can be charged with playing into the hands of the recruiters of genuine (as distinct from putative or falsely accused) terrorists. 'A new study by the intelligence consultancy Soufan Group puts the figure at approximately 5,000 fighters from EU origins' thus far recruited by Daesh, as Pierre Baussand of the Social Platform reports[7] (only two of the Paris attackers have been found to be non-European residents). Who are those young people fleeing Europe to join the terrorist cohorts and planning to return after receiving terrorist training? Baussand's well-researched and well-argued answer is that:

the majority of Western converts to Daesh come from disadvantaged backgrounds. A recent Pew Research Center study found that, 'European millennials have suffered disproportionately from their countries' recent economic troubles [. . . In the face of this challenge, young Europeans often view themselves as victims of fate.' Such widespread disenfranchisement across society goes some way to explaining the allure of the sense of importance and control that Daesh instils in its supporters.

Identifying the 'migration problem' with the problem of national and personal security, subordinating the first problem to the second and, at the end of the day, reducing the one to the other – in practice, even if not in so many words – is indeed aiding and abetting three interconnected intentions of the Al Quaedas, Daeshes and their prospective extensions and followers.

The first intention: following the logic of a self-fulfilling prophecy, to inflame anti-Islamic sentiments around Europe and so to enlist the help of the native European populations in convincing the young Muslims on the receiving end of public resentment, hostility and resulting discrimination in the countries of arrival that the gap (abyss?) separating the immigrants from their hosts is bound to remain unbridgeable – making, by the same token, the current contradictions, misunderstandings, squabbles and scuffles all that easier to extrapolate into the idea of a holy-war-to-extinction waged between the two mutually irreconcilable ways of life, or between the one and only true faith and a coalition of false creeds. Around a million young Muslims currently live in French cities, but of that number only around 1,000 have, despite strenuous efforts, been registered by French police and security services as suspected of having terrorist connections; all the same, in French public opinion, all Muslims – and particularly the young ones among them – are viewed as accessories to crime before-the-fact: believed to be guilty before any crime has been committed – thus sharing in the generic corruption and delinquency of their brothers-in-faith, becoming thereby a handy outlet for public fears and anger – regardless of their own intentions and the values they might have chosen, and however honestly and zealously they may wish, and work, to become Frenchmen in more than the formal sense of holding French passports.

The second, though closely associated, intention: following the principle of 'the worse (those young Muslims' living conditions and standing in host societies are), the better (for the terrorist cause)', to render all the more outlandish and indeed un-imaginable the prospects of a cross-cultural communication and interaction between ethnicities or religions; this would exclude in advance, or at least reduce to a minimum, the chance of a face-to-face encounter and conversation leading eventually to a mutual understanding between migrants and the nations receiving them – let alone the possibility of the absorption and integration of the immigrants into their respective host societies. Crossing out this possibility is hoped to tip even further the scale on which the young migrants weigh the attractions and repulsions of conceivable life options, in favour of joining the jihad.

Finally, the third intention is to capitalize on the dynamics of the stigma (as described in great detail by Erving Goffman in a book under the same title),[8] hoping to nourish and thrive on the implementation of the previous two. *The Merriam-Webster Dictionary* defines 'stigma' as 'a set of negative and often unfair beliefs that a society or group of people have about something', or 'a mark of shame or discredit' – in other words, a (presumably ineradicable) feature of a person or a category of persons (their weirdness, aberration, oddity and, all in all, an anomaly that makes its holders essentially different from 'us' – the 'normals', to deploy the name proposed by Goffman: 'We and those who do not depart negatively from the particular expectations at issue I shall call the *normals*' (p. 15)). Accustomed to using our own (genuine or putative) traits as the yardstick by which the humanity of other people is measured and assessed, we – the 'normals' – 'believe the person with a stigma is not quite human'. The direct outcome of all that is a blunt refusal of social acceptance and a forceful alienation of people branded as anomalous. The stigmatized persons are repelled, evicted, banished, from the group to which they might have aspired – and still, openly or deep in their hearts, aspire – but from which they have been blackballed and barred from return – after being, in addition, to add offence to injury, pressed to recognize and accept the communal verdict of their imperfection and thus inferiority: their self-inflicted failure to reach a standard on which the entry visa for the aspired-to group has been authoritatively declared dependent.

There are two possible impacts on the persons

thus stigmatized by those attaching, with public consent, the stigma. First is a painful blow delivered to the self-respect of the stigmatized person (or a person sharing in a group's allegedly generic flaw), resulting in the agonies of humiliation and shame, leading in turn to unbearable self-derogation and self-contempt and – if the stigmatized accept the verdict of the 'wider society' – ending in depression and often incapacitation. A second – apparently opposite – reaction is the perception of the stigmatization as fully undeserved, hurtful and offensive, calling for and justifying a vengeance powerful enough to reverse or effectively repeal the 'wider society's' verdict and to repossess the stolen self-respect – preferably accompanied sooner or later by the reversal of the hierarchy of worthiness proclaimed and practised by that 'wider society'.

There may be, as well, a third – we could say an intermediate and mixed – reaction: a person relatively untouched by the awareness of failing 'to live up to what we effectively demand of him', but 'insulated by his alienation, protected by identity beliefs of his own, he feels that he is a full-fledged normal human being, and that we are the ones who are not quite human' (p. 17),

Goffman suggests. Let me add, however, that – as always – being convinced of one's own 'normality' cannot be either a lonely endeavour or an individual achievement. To be *really* convincing – to disperse suspicions that this is a figment of one's imagination – the state of 'being convinced' requires a *group* affirmation, and not any group will be fit to voice it with authority; only a confirmation-by-significant-others can render the state of 'being convinced' safe and immune to the 'wider society's' opinions and actions. People who follow the pattern of the third of the above-named reactions naturally seek feverishly a group that meets those criteria – while also being ready to admit them and to vouch to guard collectively the upgraded status they claim. Recruiters to the schools for terrorists, and terrorist training camps, having rubbed their hands in joy, hasten to open their arms to the seekers.

I believe that such multifaceted – though similarly adverse and potentially lethal – consequences of the current tendency to 'securitize' the 'migration issue' and the question of admission vs rejection of refugees and asylum seekers, together with the 'guilty before the crime' stance promoted by a large part of the opinion-making media (a stance expressed for instance, from on-high, in the statement by the American Secretary of Homeland Security, Jeh Johnson, that 'the burden of proof as to whether an applicant for resettlement poses a security risk to the country falls on the individual and not on the US government. After the UN identifies a candidate for resettlement, each person still has to prove he or she is entitled to it'),[9] is topped by the rising number of governments that officially endorse the popular 'security panic' focusing on the victims of the refugee tragedy instead of on the global roots of their tragic fate. These provide between themselves the right context in which the warnings voiced recently by David Miliband, former UK Foreign Minister and now head of the International Rescue Committee, reported in the *Guardian*, need to be read and pondered:

the increasingly hostile tone of the debate on the Syrian exodus in the two western countries posed a major threat to global governance. He called on the US to honour its role as the world leader in refugee resettlement, and accused the British government of making 'a very minimal contribution' to the crisis. If America shuts itself off, especially to Muslims, that sends a huge message to the Muslim world and also to Europe. There's a ripple effect – if the west shuts down that has very serious implications.[10]

'Rather than caving in to reactionary, misinformed populist rhetoric such as that of far-right organisations, equating all migrants with terrorists', Pierre Baussand warns, 'our leaders must . . . reject "us versus them" stances and the surge in Islamophobia. This only plays into the hands of Daesh, who use such narratives as recruitment tools.' Reminding us this way that 'social exclusion is a major contributor to the radicalisation of young Muslims in the EU', and having repeated after Jean-Claude Juncker that 'those who organised these attacks and those that perpetrated them are exactly those that the refugees are fleeing and not the opposite', Baussand concludes the already-quoted statement:

While there is no doubt about the role the Muslim community must play in eradicating radicalisation, only society as a whole can tackle this common threat to us all . . . Rather than waging war on Daesh in Syria and Iraq, the biggest weapons that the West can wield against terrorism are social investment, social inclusion and integration on our own turf.[11]

This is, I suggest, a conclusion demanding our close 24/7 attention, and urgent – as well as resolute – action.

3   On Strongmen's (or Strongwomen's) Trail

A spectre is haunting the lands of democracy: the spectre of the Strongman (or Strongwoman). As Robert Reich suggests in 'Donald Trump and the Revolt of the Anxious Class',[1] that spectre (in this particular case dressed as Donald Trump, though known to be wearing many and varied local – folk, national – outfits) was born (in the style of Aphrodite emerging from the frothy tides of the Aegean Sea) of the anxiety overwhelming 'the great American middle class', now affected by the 'frighteningly high' odds 'of falling into poverty':

> Two-thirds of Americans are living paycheck to paycheck. Most could lose their jobs at any time. Many are part of a burgeoning 'on demand'

workforce – employed as needed, paid whatever they can get whenever they can get it. Yet if they don't keep up with rent or mortgage payments, or can't pay for groceries or utilities, they'll lose their footing.

Those 'two-thirds of Americans' had been forced, we could say, to walk on a sea as clobbered and buffeted by crosswinds as, and no less turbulent than, the Sea of Galilee of St Matthew's Gospel. According to that Gospel, walking on the water was a matter of keeping faith – but in whom can Reich's 'anxious class' invest their trust? 'Safety nets are full of holes. Most people who lose their jobs don't even qualify for unemployment insurance. Government won't protect their jobs from being outsourced to Asia or being taken by a worker here illegally.' As Martin Gilens and Benjamin Page, quoted by Reich, found out in 1,799 resolutions of the Congress they scrutinized, 'the preferences of the average American appear to have only a minuscule, near-zero, statistically non-significant impact upon public policy'. No wonder that more and more members of the once 'great', now 'anxious' American middle class 'view government as not so much incompetent as not giving a damn. It's working for the big guys and fat cats.' And so no wonder either that 'they'd support a strongman who'd promise to protect them from all the chaos. Who'd save jobs from being shipped abroad, slam Wall Street, stick it to China, get rid of people here illegally, and block terrorists from getting into America. A strongman who'd make America great again – which really means make average working people safe again.'

Trusting a strongman's omnipotence, Reich points out, is 'a pipe dream', and Trump's gaining of such trust is a 'conjurer's trick'. Reich's dismissal of both is, of course, correct. All the same, the rallying of the 'anxious class' around a conjurer, who tricks them into dreaming the pipe dreams he spins out, is not necessarily predetermined and inevitable. The answer to the question posited recently by Joseph M. Schwartz, Professor of Political Science at Temple University – 'Will downwardly mobile, white, middle- and working-class people follow the nativist, racist politics of Trump and Tea Partiers (who espouse the myth that the game is rigged in favor of undeserving poor people of color), or lead a charge against the corporate elites responsible for the devastation of working-class communities?'[2] – is all but a foregone conclusion. As Schwartz suggests, a *New York Times/CBS News* survey 'taken shortly before [senator Bernie] Sanders' 19 November 2015 Georgetown University speech on democratic socialism',[3] which found 56 per cent of Democratic primary voters feeling positively about socialism versus only 29 per cent who felt negatively, allows us to suppose that 'most of those polled ... associate capitalism with inequality, massive student debt and a stagnant labor market. They envision socialism to be a more egalitarian and just society.' From the present plight of the 'anxious class' (or, to deploy the concept coined by Guy Standing, of the fast-swelling – on both sides of the Atlantic – ranks of the 'precariat'), more than one policy choice derives. One policy counts on a strong man; the other on strong people.

The odds at present, however, seem far from even – and that is for a number of reasons.

In the terminology of the great Russian philosopher Mikhail Bakhtin, all earthly powers feed and thrive on recasting 'cosmic fear', inborn and endemic to humans – that is, the fear in the face of the immeasurably great and immeasurably powerful; in the face of the starry heavens, the material mass of the mountains, the sea, and the fear of cosmic upheavals and elemental disasters in ancient mythologies, worldviews, systems of images, in languages themselves and the forms of thinking bound up with them . . . This cosmic fear, fundamentally not mystical in the strict sense (being a fear in the face of the materially great and materially indefinable power), is used by all religious systems for the suppression of the person and his consciousness[4]

— into its contrived, artful 'official' variety. That recasting obviously serves the vested interest of powers-that-be; but it wouldn't do it, were it not that it simultaneously takes a step towards mitigating slightly this would-be insufferable horror — thereby rendering mundane human life a bit less unlivable; it does so by 'cutting the infinite and the timeless' down to the measure of human finite mental and pragmatic faculties. In my study *In Search of Politics*, I commented on Bakhtin's view that cosmic fear was 'the prototype of mundane, earthly power, which, however, remoulded its primeval prototype into *official* fear, the fear of the human yet not fully human power, man-made but exceeding human capacity to resist':

> [U]nlike its cosmic prototype, the official fear had to be, and indeed was, *manufactured* – designed, 'made to measure' . . . In the laws which Moses brought to the people of Israel, the echoes of thunders high up at the top of Mount Sinai reverberated. But the laws spelled out light and clear what the thunders only darkly and thus confusingly, terrifyingly, and ultimately disablingly insinuated. The laws offered answers, so that questions might cease to be asked.[5]

Out of the unmanageable – because it is infinitely distant and impenetrable – threat, a feasible, and by comparison deceptively easy, demand to obey the legibly spelled-out commandments had been conjured. Once it was brought to earth, the powers-that-be re-forged primeval fear into the horror of deviation from the rule; a superhuman cosmic tragedy into a mundane, human, all-too-human, task and duty; and the fear and trembling caused by the unfathomable enigma of God's will into the commandment to follow the intelligible, clearly spelled-out proscriptions and prescriptions collated and codified by His plenipotentiaries – His anointed spokesmen walking on earth.

In his study of the complex relationship between the earthly managers of 'official fear' and those on the receiving end of their management, and resorting to the help of *Trial* and *Castle*, Franz Kafka's two novels, Roberto Calasso shows that the issue is more complicated than this; making the 'official fear' work is not so straightforward a task.[6] 'Were the villagers to see the exegetes of *The Castle* talking long-windedly of deities and of God and how they interfere in their lives, they would probably act indignantly', Calasso suggests. They would resent all learned attempts to compare the occupants of the Castle to God, and other divine beings known to them from religious lessons. 'How simple it would be to have dealings' with the insiders of the Castle, if – as in the case of God – 'it would be enough to study a little theology and to rely upon the heart's devotion – they would think. But the Castle officials are rather more complicated. No science or discipline can help in dealing with them.'

Indeed, religious systems – according to Bakhtin the first arrangements to attempt and achieve the recycling of 'cosmic' fear into the 'official' form (or, rather, to fabricate the 'official fear' after the pattern of the 'cosmic', while capitalizing on the groundwork already done by the fear's prime, original sources) – tended to secure the submission and obedience of their subjects by promising (and delivering, even if, in quality and quantity, falling well short of what had been promised) foolproof recipes for currying God's grace and favours, and for placating His wrath in case the efforts to follow His commandments to the letter proved in practice too tough and onerous a task. Losing nothing of his fearsomeness, God might – unlike the numb and dumb sources of cosmic fear – be talked to: prayed, begged, beseeched, implored, through words and deeds, to forgive sins and reward virtues; and, unlike blind and deaf Nature, God might listen, hear, and oblige the repentant, conscience-stricken and contrite penitents. Churches, God's self-proclaimed earthly plenipotentiaries, spelled out meticulously and in profuse detail the code of conduct bound to induce Him – equipped simultaneously with the powers to bless and to curse – to do just that. Smarting under the blows of fate, the victims of God's wrath knew exactly what they had to do in order to earn redemption. If the redemption was slow in coming, they believed that they must not have been doing it zealously enough – being therefore guilty of a principally correctable misdemeanour.

But this is precisely the kind of arrangement that the modern edition of official fear, conscripted and redeployed by secular political powers, rejects in its practice – even if it hardly ever neglects to perform a lip service to its precepts. In a blatant violation of the modern intention and promise to replace the blind games of fate (that is, the annoyingly confusing disconnection of human doings from their consequences for the doers and others around them) by a coherent, relatively unambiguous order of things guided by moral principles of justice and responsibility – assuring thereby a strict correspondence between the plight of humans and their behavioural choices – humans are nowadays finding themselves exposed to a society overfilled with risks yet void of certainties and guarantees. Two novel circumstances make us rethink – and, if not revise, then at least supplement – Bakhtin's model.

The first is the far-reaching 'individualization' – a codename for the insistence of the powers-that-be who stand for the imagined totality of 'society' on 'subsidiarizing' (in simpler terms, offloading – or, yet more to the point, dumping) the task of tackling the problems generated by existential uncertainty to the eminently inadequate resources commanded by individuals on their own; as the late Ulrich Beck put it, it is now individuals who are charged with the all but unfulfillable task of finding, individually, solutions to socially produced problems.

Devoured by that diffuse, dissipated and scattered fear that infiltrates and penetrates the whole of the life setting and the totality of life-pursuits, as capillary vessels do the totality of the living body, humans are abandoned to their own resources – puny and miserably flimsy assets by comparison with the grandiosity of existential liabilities. As Byung-Chul Han suggests,[7] Kafka himself supplied the key to his heroes' condition in his concise aphorism that contained a new interpretation of the Prometheus legend,[8] 'Gods are tired, vultures are tired, liver closed up tired' – adding that nowadays the semiotics of the liver pain is that of fatigue: weariness, exhaustion, incapacitation; and that it is we, the denizens and actors-by-behest of the present-day 'society of performance' – now deputizing for the old-fashioned 'society of discipline', while replacing the Freudian watchword *devoir* with *pouvoir* in the office of its *mot d'ordre* – who are manoeuvred into the function of vultures causing that fatigue (pp. 7–9). Holding to Byung-Chul Han's metaphorics, we need to conclude that, as long as our *mots d'ordre* are no longer obedience, law and obligations to be met, but liberty, desires and a penchant for enjoying their satisfaction (p. 12), our plight is a DIY version of the Promethean drama. We are the liver torn apart, and we are the vultures tearing it apart. Taking a leaf from Alain Ehrenberg's *La Fatigue d'être soi*,[9] Byung-Chul Han proposes that depression, the staple ailment in a society of performers, is not caused by the excess of responsibilities and duties, but by the 'imperative of performance, the novel rule of the society of post-modern labour'.[10]

How is this happening? This time over, it is in a way starkly different from that remembered from the 'society of discipline' (in my terms, the 'solid modern' society) immortalized by Franz Kafka or Michel Foucault – a society used to sedimenting and expurgating criminals such as Joseph K. from Kafka's *Trial*, and/or lunatics as in Foucault's doctoral dissertation *Folie*

et déraison. Histoire de la folie à l'âge classique.
As Byung-Chul Han suggests, our 'society of
performance' specializes, for a change, in the
manufacture and purging of 'depressives and
misfits' (p. 52). Failing to reach the standards
and volumes of performance that the denizens
of the 'society of performance' are expected to
attain and must attain in order to survive (often
bodily, but always socially), both above-named
categories fall victim to self-exploitation, self-
tormenting and self-exhaustion. They both are
simultaneously victims and culprits of their failure and of the depression that, at the same time,
causes and follows it (cf. p. 56). It is their own
shameful inadequacy, stripping them of whatever
has remained of their self-esteem, that they blame
for their misfortune and humiliation.

The 'society of performance' is, first and foremost, a society of *individual* performance, and
of a 'culture of sink-or-swim individualism' – in
which 'daily life becomes precarious', forcing the
individual into a 'state of constant readiness';
'Predictable income, savings, the fixed category
of "occupation", all belong to another historical world'[11] under the 'form of governing that at
least since Thomas Hobbes has been viewed as no

longer possible: a government that is not legitimized by promising protection and security'.[12] With the powers on-high washing their hands of the duty to make lives livable, the uncertainties of human existence are privatized, responsibility for tackling them is cast fairly and squarely on the wan individual's shoulders, while existential oppressions and calamities are dismissed as DIY jobs foolishly perpetrated by their sufferers. Doomed to seek individually designed and individually manageable solutions to problems generated by society going back on its earlier promises and now relentlessly retreating from the pledge to endorse a collective insurance against the hazards of individual life, the individual is abandoned to her or his individual resources, all too often found sorely inadequate – or feared soon to be found as such. For the individual cast onto the abandoned and vacated part of the trajectory of the state's retreat, 'individualization' portends a new precarity of the existential condition: a leap from the frying pan into the fire: 'Governmental precarization . . . means not only destabilization through employment, but also destabilization of the conduct of life.'[13] Fear of being branded non-conforming, officially disseminated and cultivated in the society of discipline, has, in the society of performance, been replaced by the fear of inadequacy. All in all, officially 'emancipated' individuals find themselves not up to the trials and tribulations of the thoroughly individualized life.

The spectre hovering over a society of would-be performers-by-decree is the horror of finding oneself deficient – inept and inefficacious – as well as the terror of its immediate effects – loss of self-esteem and its probable sequels: black-balling, out-casting and exclusion. As generators of official fear, the power-holders keep busy to beef up the existential uncertainty from which that spectre has risen and is perpetually reborn; power-holders are eager to do everything conceivable to render that spectre as tangible and credible – as 'realistic' – as possible; after all, the official fear of their subjects is what, in the last instance, keeps them in power. However, in a society pulverized into an aggregate of individual performers (forced to pretend to be self-reliant), the holders of power can look forward to relying increasingly on us – their unpaid, insecure, precarious and unprotected interns, carrying out fragmented life in a society whose fragmentation they support and reproduce daily.

Having passed through the religious and political incarnations of the 'official fear' of the 'society of discipline', cosmic fear emanating from the agonizing finitude and thinness of human cognitive and pragmatic powers descended, in the 'society of performers', into the realm of 'life politics' (Anthony Giddens' term), and landed on the shoulders of that life's individual practitioners. Crammed between the infinity of allegedly accessible options and temptations as well as the boundlessness of demands addressed to the individual, who is assumed to be 'autonomous, potent, strong willed' and nudged to be 'relentlessly striving to improve' herself or himself,[14] on one side, and the meagreness of the individually managed resources forced into view by the sheer grandiosity of that challenge, on the other, the performers-by-decree, harassed by the awareness of their own inadequacy, have left little option except to appeal for salvation from impending depression to 'gods of their own' – as Ulrich Beck memorably suggested, 'gods of one's own choosing'.[15] This switch of allegiance has done little, however, to mitigate either the harrowing anxiety emanating from the all-too-obvious precarity of their existential status, or the pains of self-censure and self-condemnation for failing to arrest – let alone to reverse – its further deterioration.

The second novel circumstance is the erosion of the territorial sovereignty of the extant political units, caused by the on-going process of the globalization of power (i.e., the capability to have things done) *not* being followed by a similar globalization of politics (i.e., the capability to decide what things need to be done), and resulting therefore in a jarring discrepancy between the objectives and the means of effective action. The outcome is the departure of the sources of 'official fear' from the model sketched by Bakhtin: invisible and unattainable for most intents and purposes, they are now – just like the sources of 'cosmic fear' – all but numb and dumb. At a lofty distance from the petitioners, they are immune to their petitions, let alone their demands. Most of their subjects are cut off from communication – and more and more of them have lost, or are fast losing, all hope of sensible conversation with the powers-that-be.

Eric Hobsbawm, one of the most perspicacious historians of the modern era, intimated a quarter of a century ago (and so, well before the present 'migration crisis' took off, or even the present awareness of the novel 'globality' of the human condition) that

> urbanization and industrialization, resting as they do on massive and multifarious movements, migration and transfer of people, undermine the basic nationalist assumption of a territory inhabited essentially by an ethnically, culturally and linguistically homogeneous population. The sharp xenophobic or racist reaction of the native population in receiving countries or regions to the massive influx of 'strangers' has been, unfortunately, familiar in the USA since the 1890s and in Western Europe since the 1960s. Yet xenophobia and racism are symptoms, not cures. Ethnic communities and groups in modern societies are fated to coexist, whatever the rhetoric which dreams of a return to an unmixed nation.

Today, 'the typical "national minority" in most countries receiving migration, is an archipelago of small islands rather than a coherent land-mass.' 'Time and again', Hobsbawm added, 'movements of ethnic identity seem to be reactions of weakness and fear, attempts to erect barricades to keep at bay the forces of the modern world

. . . What fuels such defensive reactions, whether against real or imaginary threats, is a combination of international population movements with the ultra-rapid, fundamental and unprecedented socio-economic transformations' still so characteristic of our times; 'Wherever we live in an urbanized society, we encounter strangers: uprooted men and women who remind us of the fragility or the drying up of our own families' roots.' Hobsbawm quoted Czech analyst Miroslav Hroch to the effect that nationalism and ethnicity are 'a substitute for factors of integration in a disintegrating society. When society fails, the nation appears as the ultimate guarantee.' 'They' (the 'strangers'), as Hobsbawm reminds us from beyond his grave, 'can be, must be, blamed for all the grievances, uncertainties and disorientations which so many of us feel after forty years of the most rapid and profound upheavals of human life in recorded history'. As our ancient ancestors insisted but we are recklessly forgetting, to our own detriment, 'history is the teacher of life'. For the sake of our survival, let's listen to that teacher: let's read and re-read Eric Hobsbawm's trail-blazing *Nations and Nationalism since 1780*. The lesson we can draw from that great book is that failing societies that invest their hopes in a saviour, a man (or woman) of providence, are looking for someone staunchly, militantly, pugnaciously nationalistic: someone who promises to shut out the globalized planet, to lock the doors that long ago lost their hinges (or, rather, had them broken), thereby becoming useless.

But – as Benjamin Barber puts it bluntly in his equally provocative and convincing-sounding study/manifesto published in 2014 by Yale University Press under the title *If Mayors Ruled the World: Dysfunctional Nations, Rising Cities* – 'Today, after a long history of regional success, the nation-state is failing us on the global scale. It was the perfect political recipe for the liberty and independence of autonomous peoples and nations. It is utterly unsuited to interdependence.' 'Too inclined by their nature to rivalry and mutual exclusion', they appear 'quintessentially indisposed to cooperation and incapable of establishing global common goods'. And yet, as Ulrich Beck put it in *Cosmopolitan Vision*,[16] even if '"cosmopolitans" are to this day regarded in many countries as something between vagabonds, enemies and insects who can or even must be banished, demonised or destroyed' (p. 3), we are all already living, whether we like it or not, on a 'cosmopolitanized' planet with porous and highly osmotic borders and universal interdependence. What we are lacking is 'cosmopolitan awareness' to match our cosmopolitan condition. I would add: we also lack the political institutions capable of making words flesh. William F. Ogburn, were he still among us, could have used our present situation as the pre-eminent – indeed cardinal – illustration for his theory of 'cultural lag', published in 1922 under the ambitious title *Social Change*.

It is for those reasons spelled out above that Robert Reich is correct when he labels as a 'pipe dream' the pledges by Donald Trump (and, by proxy, by those of his growing ilk) to put things right by barring the import and enforcing the export of foreigners, and brands their electoral career as a 'conjurer's trick'. The point, though, is that, before their frustrated constituency debunks those promises and performances as such, much water is likely to flow under increasingly decrepit and rickety bridges for the still local politics struggling to catch up with already global powers. The truth is that the shortcuts suggested by aspiring strongmen and strongwomen are no less seductive for being mis-leading. Fraudulent the promises might be, but they are catchy and seductive; they paint a vision of restoring and re-appropriating everything that a great and growing number of our contemporaries miss in the present-day politics that is known to suffer a steadily increasing deficit of power, and for that reason demonstrates its incapacity to prevent the damage done by the powers that evade its control and ignore, as well as nipping in the bud, all (though, to be sure, they are rare and far between) attempts by liberal-democratic politicians to regain their dwindling authority. The unforgivable sin of democracy, in the eyes of a growing number of its supposed beneficiaries, is its failure to deliver, and its seeking of an excuse for that failure in the formula 'TINA' ('There Is No Alternative'), meaning 'we can't do otherwise'; the concept of 'parliament', after all, is a derivative of *parler* ('speaking', 'talking') – not of 'having things done'. The attraction of the pretenders to a strongman's or strongwoman's role consists in their *pledge to act* – even if their only action for the time being is speaking and talking – as well as in the fact that what they tend to speak and talk about is that they *can* do otherwise, that there *is* an alternative: that they *are* that alternative; finally, the strongmen's and strongwomen's seductive powers rest on all those pledges and pretensions remaining untested.

4 Together and Crowded

The first humans, similarly to the hominids from which they branched, were hunters and gatherers, and for that reason must have been nomads; their progeny, the *Homo sapiens* species, remained nomads for most of their later history. Historian William McNeill judges that 'it is safe to assume that when our ancestors first became fully human they were already migratory, moving about in pursuit of big game'.[1] Between 2 and 1.5 million years ago, the genus named *Homo* branched off from the already bipedal, 2 million years more ancient, *Australopithecus*. Both species were innately, intrinsically migratory.

The first migrations of our ancestors are thought to have been confined to the African continent – while 100,000 years ago some of

their progeny, considered by palaeontologists
to already belong to the *Homo sapiens* species,
are believed to have moved from Africa to the
Near East, and from there dispersed to all con-
tinents of the globe; they were migrants through
and through – migration, as Kevin Kenny sums
up, 'was built into their mode of life'. The history of the human species has known quite a
few massive translocations and dislocations of
large parts or totalities of entire societies. And,
according to Kevin Kenny's collation of the most
recent scholarly findings, 'everyone alive today
is descended from a small group of anatomically
modern humans' of East African origin; 'Recent
genetic studies demonstrate that mitochon-
dria within human cells descend from a single
woman', baptized retrospectively as the 'African
Eve', who lived in Africa at some time between
200,000 and 150,000 years ago.[2] Even if there
is – as the reports arriving from the frontlines of
the current process recorded as the 'immigration
crisis' (a codename, let me suggest, as vague as it
is portentous and intentionally alarming) imply
– something strikingly novel in the origin of the
present-day massive dislocation of people, there
is, however, little if anything unprecedented in

the pattern of social/political responses to it, as I am trying to show.

Important, seminal changes in *human modes of cohabitation*, however, have occurred – among many, the steadily (though in leaps and bounds) rising density of human inhabitation of the planet: physical density alongside the spiritual.

'For most of our history', as Kwame Anthony Appiah pointed out, our ancestors 'would see, on a typical day, only people [they] had known' most of their lives.[3] All their clothes and tools – indeed, all the artefacts they saw and used daily – were made by such people; 'That is the world that shaped us, the world in which our nature was formed.' It was not that long ago – indeed, a minuscule snip of human history ago – that we managed somehow 'to live cheek by jowl in societies where most of those who spoke your language and shared your laws and grew the food on your table were people you would never know'. 'Only in the past couple of centuries have we come to a point where each of us can realistically imagine contacting any other' of the rest of the 7 billion human inhabitants of planet Earth. We can share with them some of the things we have made and cherish but they miss and crave – and we can force on them things that we have made but they detest and abhor; and what applies to us, applies equally to them. Appiah concludes: the challenge 'is to take minds and hearts formed over the long millennia of living in local troops and equip them with ideas and institutions that will allow us to live together as the global tribe we have become'. A great challenge indeed; fully and truly a life-and-death (*joint* life, *joint* death) challenge. Approaching (or perhaps having reached already) a fork in the path to our possible futures, one track aimed at cooperative well-being and the other leading to collective extinction, we are still unable to raise our awareness, intentions and deeds to the already existing – and utterly unlikely to reverse – globality of our species-wide interdependence: a condition that makes the choice between survival and extinction dependent on our capability to 'live cheek and jowl', in mutual peace, solidarity and cooperation, amidst strangers who may or may not hold opinions and preferences similar to ours.

There are no empty lands left on the planet for colonizing; what is more, there are no lands left which could be imagined and treated as such by aspiring colonizers boasting a power great enough to force them open to newcomers by cleansing them of their indigenous population. Kant predicted the advent of such a situation, well before it happened. And he ruminated on the 'imperatives' which would need to be observed once that happened – as happen it must. How to live together – live *in peace* – on a *full* planet reaching the limits of its accommodating capacity?

In his *Third Definitive Article for a Perpetual Peace* (spelled out as 'The Law of World Citizenship Shall Be Limited to Conditions of Universal Hospitality'), Kant insists that the issue he writes about, and what he writes about it,

is not a question of philanthropy but of right. Hospitality means the right of a stranger not to be treated as an enemy when he arrives in the land of another. One may refuse to receive him when this can be done without causing his destruction; but, so long as he peacefully occupies his place, one may not treat him with hostility. It is not the right to be a permanent visitor that one may demand. A special beneficent agreement would be needed in order to give an outsider a right to become a fellow inhabitant for a certain length of time. It is only a right of temporary sojourn, a right to associate, which all men have. They have it by virtue of their common possession of the surface of the earth, where, as a globe, they cannot infinitely disperse and hence must finally tolerate the presence of each other. Originally, no one had more right than another to a particular part of the earth.[4]

Let's note Kant's caution – and the circumspection with which he articulates the conditions of the world-wide 'perpetual peace' on a globe on which its inhabitants 'cannot infinitely disperse and hence must finally tolerate the presence of each other'. What Kant demands is not the cancellation of the distinction between lands (countries – territorially sovereign and self-governing states, viewed and treated by their respective populations as their rightful homelands), but 'a right to associate' (to communicate, to enter into friendly interaction, and eventually to try to establish mutually beneficial bonds of friendship, presumed to be spiritually enriching); what Kant demands is the substitution of *hospitality* for *hostility*. In the principle of mutual hospitality Kant gleaned the possibility, and a prospect, of universal peace putting an end to the long history of internecine wars tearing apart the European continent.

More than 200 years and several bloody wars later, we are still procrastinating in attending to Kant's appeal to hospitality. As David Miliband commented in the previously quoted interview:

Offers of help from the US and UK governments were inadequate . . . The British government has said it will take 4,000 Syrians a year – equivalent to the number that arrived in the Greek island of Lesbos in a single day . . . Were that number to be stepped up to 25,000 a year, that would still amount to only 40 refugees per parliamentary constituency – for instance of South Shields [Miliband's old seat]. Is anyone going to argue that South Shields couldn't cope with 40 people from Syria? That argument's not sustainable . . . Britain is a country that has provided a haven for people across generations and benefited from refugees playing all sorts of roles in national life. When the UK keeps the door only slightly ajar, that sends a message that it's OK to shut the door totally to those who would go further.

Here, we are in the realm of *rights and duties* (things which *morality* relates to, concerns itself with and aspires to codify) – not in the realm of the *'facts of life'*, the domain that *politics* administrates and aspires to rule. Of that distinction Immanuel Kant had the following to say, in the First Appendix to the essay titled 'On the Opposition between Morality and Politics with respect to Perpetual Peace':

> Politics says, 'Be ye wise as serpents'; morality adds, as a limiting condition, 'and guileless as doves'. If these two injunctions are incompatible in a single command, then politics and morality are really in conflict; but if these two qualities ought always to be united, the thought of contrariety is absurd, and the question as to how the conflict between morals and politics is to be resolved cannot even be posed as a problem.

Two centuries later, Emmanuel Levinas would take a more partisan (and radical) stance, when, in the on-going *querelle* between morality and ontology (that is, the postulated domain of politics' concerns and administration), he assigned priority, unambiguously and unconditionally, to ethics. It is ontology (the human existential condition, which includes society, the object of political administration) that needs to (is due to, ought to, and should) submit itself to the evaluation and judgement of ethics – not the other way round.

Contrary to the etymological pedigree of the concept of morality, ethics is *not* a collection of *mores* (acquired usages, habits and manners, currently accepted – yet expendable – behavioural patterns, commonly held opinions – which could be, as Hannah Arendt repeatedly intimated shortly before her death, 'exchanged for another set with hardly more trouble than it would take to change the table manners of an individual or a people') – mores reflecting the 'will of society' as it is at a given time, though it could be different in another. It is also contrary to the postulate of Friedrich Nietzsche, who, when appealing to 'devalue all extant values' and urging us to search for new ones to replace them, called for life to be recognized as the highest good, whereas 'all ethics, Christian or non-Christian, presuppose that life is *not* the highest good for mortal men and that there is always more at stake in life than sustenance and procreation of individual living organisms' – as Arendt emphatically averred in her posthumously collated and published 'Some Questions of Moral Philosophy',[5] her long and thoughtful conversation with Immanuel Kant, conducted over 200 years after Kant asked his fundamental questions, to which Arendt tried to give updated answers with the benefit of historical evidence whose content Kant could only have guessed at. As Arendt bitterly observes, 'the only new principle, proclaimed in modern times, turns out to be not the assertion of "new values", but the negation of morality as such'.

It seems, however, that it is not the 'negation of morality as such' that constitutes the most awesome of menaces threatening the ethical standards on which our shared residence on the globalizing planet is (or, more precisely, could be, and ought to struggle to become) grounded. Few, if any, authoritative sources voice nowadays – and fewer still admit to propagating – the futility of moral convictions and of their observance; these days, wars are waged and fought under the banner of sacrosanct ethical principles, whether they are deemed to be of divine origin or inherent to *Homines sapientes* armed by logic, assisted, prodded and operated by reason. The most daunting and horrifying of the manifold dangers to morality lies elsewhere: in the stealthily, but steadily and relentlessly, expanding territory of 'adiaphorization': of the area of human interrelationships and interaction exempted from moral evaluation – and consequently treated in practice as 'morally indifferent', 'beyond good and evil', subject solely to assessment by its efficiency in 'bringing results'. 'Be ye wise as serpents' – the sole precept that is obeyed by and demanded of a politics focused on getting results – is in a rising number of cases *not* accompanied by the prerequisite of being 'guileless as doves', that codicil that morality would wish – were it allowed – to add. And let us note, with Hannah Arendt, that for quite a long time already this stance has *not* been a monopoly of those at the helm, or even of a special category of professional practitioners of the political craft, trained and drilled, groomed and honed into an ideologically inspired moral blindness, and all in all effectively immunized against everything irrelevant to the success of the task at hand – including the costs paid in the currency of human suffering and abasement: 'No one had to be a convinced Nazi to conform, and to forget overnight, as it were, not his social status, but

the moral convictions which once went with it'
(p. 54).

What is currently happening – in stark opposition to the steadily expanding space of human
interdependence – is the constriction of that
realm of moral obligations that we are ready
to admit, take responsibility for, and accept as
the object of our constant, daily attention and
remedial action: not only for the duration of the
notoriously short-lived carnivalesque explosions
of solidarity and care that are triggered by media
images of successive spectacular tragedies in the
migrants' unending saga. The snag is that, for the
lengthy time spans separating such moral car-
nivals, we tend to live in a world sharply, and
apparently irreparably, split into 'us' and 'them'.
Such a fissure does not require a 'negation of
morality as such'. On the contrary, daily, and on
a massive scale, that rift spawns frantic efforts to
draft moral impulses – never dead, but most of
the time put to sleep – into the service of social
and political division and antagonism.

As it were, 'morality' is far from becoming in
our times a derogatory or derisory attribute; now,
as before, 'morality' is a name for a property that
is widely coveted, that people wish to appropri-

ate, possess and (jealously) guard – if not for any other reason, then surely for the sake of the authority it's hoped it will bestow on those who claim it, of the hoped-for assistance it may offer to the recruiting officers chasing recruits and proselytizers in search of would-be converts, of the advantages it may bring 'us' over 'them', and of the endorsement of our action we expect from claiming moral superiority over our competitors and adversaries. The right to the label 'moral' is for all those reasons 'essentially contested' by mutually antagonistic power camps. Each side of the frontline would hotly deny all and any suspicion of moral indifference, moral blindness or an immoral stance; and each would be all too eager to charge 'them', as distinct from 'us', with all those perversions.

Being moral means, in the nutshell, knowing the difference between good and evil and where to draw a line between them – as well as being able to tell one from another when you watch them in action or contemplate enacting them. By extension, it also means recognizing one's own (as universal as it is absolute and unconditional, as Levinas insisted) responsibility for promoting good and resisting evil. In the practice of morally informed/stimulated conduct, however, drawing limits to that responsibility (cutting it down to the size of the possible, affordable, attainable and, all in all, 'realistic') all too often proves to be inescapable. An absolute, unlimited and unexceptional responsibility for the well-being of an-Other (and so presumably for *all* others) might be a commandment made to the measure of saints – a rule to which only saints could fully and perpetually submit with no exceptions (or at least would attempt such a submission). Few of us can, however, claim to possess saintly qualities; it is therefore an unavoidable task, and inalienable mission of society, to cut the absolute responsibility to the measure of ordinary ('average') human creatures and their realistic capabilities: to set limits on how far acting on that responsibility (the fulfilment of moral duty) must go to avoid sliding into its opposite, the state of moral blindness. That much is inescapable. What is, however, principally avoidable (and so, from the ethical point of view, needs to be by all means averted and eschewed) is the common tendency for human societies to set limits also on the aggregate of human creatures to whose treatment moral responsibilities must be applied: in other words, the exemption of certain categories of other humans from the realm of moral obligation. If the first limitation is endemic to the state of moral responsibility due to its absoluteness, the second cannot be reconciled with it and needs to be seen and treated as its violation, enforced 'from without', by forces and for reasons foreign to moral concerns and considerations. To put it bluntly: what is wholly and unconditionally alien to the quality of 'being moral', and what militates against it, is the tendency to halt and renounce moral responsibility for others at the border drawn between 'us' and 'them'.

Confrontation between the unconditional nature of moral responsibility and its rejection or neglect in the case of some humans, also its natural objects, cannot but cause a cognitive dissonance – a disturbing, noxious state of mind and will: a phenomenon common in the case of confusing yet irresolvable ambivalence of perception and behaviour. Leon Festinger, who articulated that phenomenon and coined its name,[6] produced a list of stratagems to which affected people resort in seeking (consciously or not) a way to mitigate that perceptive ambivalence and to disperse the behavioural confusion it causes. The most common ploy is to diminish, or preferably deny altogether, the validity of one of the mutually contradictory perceptions – or at least to minimize or completely eliminate its persuasive power. When applied to the case under discussion here, this ploy takes the form of ascribing to people exempted from our (otherwise unconditional) moral responsibility features that besmirch and defame their image; of re-presenting such categories of humans as unworthy of regard and respect, and thus justifying our disregard and lack of care as a deserved punishment for the incurable vices or vicious intentions of those whom we have disregarded and ignored, harshly treated or callously neglected.

The concept of cognitive dissonance and its expectable sequels goes a long way towards explaining and making intelligible the otherwise recondite meanderings of European reactions to the influx of asylum-seeking refugees. These people have been variously accused of carrying terminal diseases, being in the service of Al Qaeda or the 'Islamic State', intending to sponge on (the remnants of) the European welfare system, or scheming to convert Europe to Islam and impose the rule of sharia law. These are just a few off-the-cuff illustrations among many, and are still growing daily in number:

In his latest outburst Czech President Milos Zeman accused wealthy economic migrants of cynically exploiting children to reach the European Union. 'They serve as human shields for guys with iPhones to justify the wave of migrants.' 'Those hiding behind the children . . . in my opinion, do not deserve any compassion.' 'They bring the children over in rubber dinghys, knowing they might drown', said Zeman, in office since 2013 as the Czech Republic's first-ever directly elected president. The statements follow his earlier fiery remarks targeting refugees, including 'no one invited you here'. Zeman also recently said migrants would 'respect sharia (Islamic law) instead of Czech laws' and that 'unfaithful women will be stoned and thieves will have their hands cut off'.[7]

The overall effect of these and similar imputations, slanders and calumnies (as a rule, poorly – if at all – supported by facts) is, first of all, the dehumanization of incomers (casting them, by design or by default, in the category of *Homini sacri* – that is, in Giorgio Agamben's terminology, persons stripped of both lay and religious significance and value). Dehumanization paves the way for their exclusion from the category of legitimate human rights-holders and leads, with dire consequences, to the shifting of the migration issue from the sphere of ethics to that of threats to security, crime prevention and punishment, criminality, defence of order, and, all in all, the state of emergency usually associated with the threat of military aggression and hostilities.[8]

Proofs of this tendency are by no means difficult to come by. In the *Daily Mail*, for instance, Dominic Sandbrook rebukes the (in his view, unacceptably lenient) stand of the British Prime Minister: 'Mr Cameron's predecessors managed to keep out Napoleon and Hitler, both of whom had gigantic armies and an entire continent behind them. So he really should be able to cope with a few thousand exhausted migrants – shouldn't he?' And this is how Emma Barnett, the Women's Editor of the *Daily Telegraph*, describes the dominant trend in the presentation of migrants by the opinion-making media:

Even the language that's being used to describe the mostly male Eritreans, Ethiopians, Afghans and

Sudanese trying to live in Europe is mechanical at best, and dehumanising at worst. Emergency government meetings are being held to ensure there is 'upstream management of illegal migratory flows.' Excuse me? These are real people, with hearts, families and lest we forget it, human rights.

Meanwhile, Sid Miller, the Agriculture Commissioner in the wealthy state of Texas, compares Syrian refugees to rattlesnakes, posting on Facebook images of snakes and refugees and asking, 'Can you tell me which of these rattlers won't bite you?' His superior, Governor Greg Abbott, tells reporters that 'we cannot allow charity for some to compromise the safety for all'.[9] And last, though not necessarily least: the information that 'Katie Hopkins will not face charges over allegations that she incited racial hatred in a newspaper article calling migrants "cockroaches" [the name, by the way, given by the attackers to their victims during the Rwandan genocide], and "feral humans"', as well as over publishing an article with the title 'Rescue Boats? I'll Use Gunboats to Stop Migrants', was printed by the already-quoted *Mail* under the heading 'Cops Get Attack of Common Sense at Last.'[10]

5   Troublesome, Annoying, Unwanted: Inadmissible

Even George Konrad, a man who once fought to topple the communist regime in Hungary under the banner of liberalism – a man described by the *New York Times* as 'a veteran of communist-era struggles against dictatorship' who 'loathes his country's stridently illiberal prime minister, Viktor Orban'[1] – has declared that, though Orban 'is not a good democrat and I don't believe he is a good person', when it comes to his policy towards immigrants (that is, sealing the borders, building fences and sounding the alarm about the perils they portend), 'it hurts to admit it, but . . . he was right'. In other words: what is wrong with Orban is that he is illiberal towards the citizens of the country he rules; but what is right is that he is illiberal towards people who seek in that country salvation from tyranny and gory persecution, and/or inhuman poverty.

The same *New York Times* report informs us that, during their final summit meeting of 2015 (on 17 December), European leaders had 'begun to echo' Orban, 'though without his nasty snarls' (which means they hid their message – cravenly, even if sanctimoniously – behind the veil of a 'politically correct' vocabulary). What they discussed and attempted to resolve, under the heading of the 'migration problem', was in the last account (and, in fact, in its essence) the need to 'regain control' of the continent's frontiers. Having adopted the precept of *deux poids, deux mesures* meant originally for one of the member states – Hungary – they raised it to the rank of an all-European canon.

Michel Agier – perhaps the most incisive, consistent and, by now, by far the most experienced and knowledgeable researcher into the fate of over 200 million persons currently (globally) displaced – suggests that the 'migration policy' is aimed at 'consolidating a partition between two great world categories that are increasingly reified: on the one hand, a clean, healthy and visible world; on the other, the world of residual "remnants", dark, diseased and invisible'. He anticipates that, if practices go on as they currently do, that aim will overwhelm and dwarf all other ostensible concerns and functions: camps 'will no longer be used to keep vulnerable refugees alive, but rather to park and guard all kinds of undesirable populations'.[2]

The presence of 'remnants' is a worldwide, not just Europe-confined, phenomenon. That term refers to people left out of our sight, concern and conscience – born and bred as we are amidst the comforts and conveniences of the world: we, who live in homes, not under tents and inside the barracks of refugees' or asylum-seekers' camps. The 'remnants' populate 'countless camps, kilometres of transit corridors, islands and marine platforms, and enclosures in the middle of deserts'; 'Each camp is encircled by walls, barbed wire and electric fences, or imprisoned simply by the dissuasive presence of the emptiness surrounding it.' If they manage to visit our world, 'their entries and exits are made through narrow corridors, under the filter of cameras, fingerprint readers, detectors for weapons, viruses and bacteria, captors of thoughts and memories' (pp. 1–2). If we have suddenly noticed their presence, it has

happened mostly because we discovered the previously overlooked and all-but-ignored conduit
linking the 'two great world categories': a pas-
sage not plugged tightly enough by the previous
(now found to be evidently insufficient) efforts
to keep the two categories apart and at a safe
(read: 'impassable') distance from each other. It
is not that we suddenly resolved to take off our
blinders because we had been prodded by pangs
of conscience – it is, rather, that we have been
forced by 'remnants', appearing on our doorstep
en masse, to confront eye to eye the previously
comfortingly, consolingly invisible aspects of the
state-of-the-world reality. That mass clogged the
'narrow corridors' and blocked their 'entries and
exits'; our refined high-tech filters, detectors and
captors, designed and made to service the coming
and going of 'occasional visitors', have been discredited and promptly proclaimed outdated and
useless for being demonstratively unable to do
their job of filtering, detecting and capturing
when confronted with dozens, and hundreds, of
thousands of 'remnants'.

Don Flynn, the Director of the Migrants'
Rights Network, suggests that the year 2015
'will come to be seen as the year in which the

movement of people into and out of the country became finally and indissolubly Europeanised'.[3] He also suggests that this development could possibly be a good thing, 'with progressive, forward-thinking governments working together to see how the movement of people is going to play its role in promoting sustainable growth and the welfare of populations, while at the same time cementing human rights and fairness right the way across the system'. No less weighty signs, however, abound, indicating that following the above-portrayed scenario is in no way a foregone conclusion – things may well turn in the opposite direction. Flynn admits that much, qualifying his optimistic prognosis with the observation that:

Sadly this isn't the way in which immigration has been considered by governments for a long time. The resulting dysfunction has meant that Europe has become associated in the minds of many with turmoil and threat. The image of desperate refugees landing on the Greek islands; the bodies of children washed up on holiday beaches; people pushed back by thuggish police action on the borders of Hungary; or the migrants living in the squalor of the 'jungle' camps in Calais will probably be the abiding memories of the past year for many.

While Germany 'initiated an extraordinary few weeks in which hundreds of thousands of citizens were suddenly released from a mind-set which told them to fear and loathe migrants and instead to offer them a welcome', the Prime Minister of Great Britain, 'despite the absence of any evidence that the migration of EU citizens constituted a major problem for national welfare systems . . . decided that it is a major issue which requires urgent resolution . . . [Despite the fact that] people exercising free movement rights are net contributors to the welfare system, as any number of independent reports have shown'. Prospects for the coming year(s) vacillate between 'immigration continuing to look like permanent guerrilla warfare aimed at reducing the rights of migrants and keeping them in a state of insecurity and vulnerability', and 'winning greater support for a rights-based approach to the management of migration'.

The 'Europeanization' of the 'migration issue', currently the officially accepted policy of the European Union, is at the moment being energetically pursued – though that does not necessarily augur, let alone assure, a move towards the 'rights-based approach' that Flynn anticipated. On the *BBC News* of 19 December 2015, Laurence Peter entitled his report 'Migrant Crisis: EU Border Security Becomes New Mantra'. What he reported is that:

> EU leaders agreed on the need for a new 'European Border and Coast Guard', with greater powers and resources than the current Frontex border agency. The European Commission stressed that the new force would not usurp the authority of national border staff – it would work alongside them. Controversially, however, if a member state fails in its duty to protect the EU's external borders, during an emergency, the Commission could deploy EU guards without needing the state's permission. And part of the guards' remit would be to send failed asylum seekers back – though currently such 'returns' are handled by national forces.

No wonder that the Centre for European Policy Studies (CEPS) criticized the agreement for being the product of an approach to migrant aid that is 'too security-focused' to help 'tackle the root causes, especially poverty'. The money allocated to be transferred to the African countries at the root of the 'migration crisis' is meant to be used primarily for installation of camps where the prospective migrants to Europe are to be accommodated (and closely guarded), and pre-selection of inmates with no chance of asylum (who will be barred from proceeding on their way to Europe) is to be conducted. 'Root countries' are thereby included in Europe's concern with border-building to stem the migration – but references to the 'root causes' of migration are few and far between, accorded only a secondary importance.

The agreement to shift a large part of the endeavour to reinforcing 'European borders' was all but unanimous, but at this point unanimity between EU member states grinds to a halt. According to a brief summary of the current state of European practices and intentions by Alan Travers – the Home Affairs Correspondent of the *Guardian* –

A French-based IFOP poll of seven countries showed support for the principle of sheltering refugees from war and persecution has dropped in Germany from 79% in September to 75% in

October. Fewer than half of Britons, French or Dutch say they feel the same way. While the demand for an upper limit on the number of refugees in Germany has damaged Merkel, it seems far from sweeping her from office. David Cameron and his home secretary, Theresa May, on the other hand, have not only kept the door firmly shut but have made a virtue of it. While Germany accepted 108,000 asylum seekers between September and November, Cameron was boasting last week of resettling just 1,000 Syrian refugees over a longer period. The PM has firmly argued that it is better to keep the 4 million Syrian refugees 'in-region', underpinned by a generous cumulative £1bn aid programme and to end the incentive for those making the journey by 'breaking the link between getting on a boat in the Mediterranean and getting the right to settle in Europe'.[4]

In paying lip service to the 'Europeanization' of the migration problem while exempting his own country from sharing in the duties that follow, Cameron is not alone. Travers cites the example of Denmark: 'Countries such as Denmark dropped their previous pledges to take part in the relocation programme as politicians proposed seizing refugees' jewellery and cash. It is a measure of Europe's failure that so far only 160 or so of the one million refugees who made it to Europe by sea or by land have been relocated under the scheme.' Even the countries most in the limelight as forthcoming and active in saving the shipwrecked victims of criminal smugglers wishing to profit from human tragedy react to the tragedies *after* they happen, while stopping well short of striving to prevent them from happening:

> Currently, the EU offers Syrians the prospect of heaven (life in Germany), but only if they first pay a crook and risk their lives. Only 2 percent succumb to this temptation, but inevitably in the process thousands drown. This policy is so irresponsible that it is morally closer to the recklessness of manslaughter than to the virtue of rescue. It showers fortune on the few, kills thousands, and ignores millions.[5]

6 Anthropological vs Time-bound Roots of Hatred

Kant believed that moral knowledge, the knowledge of right and wrong, is given to all humans, thanks to every human's rational faculties. He was not so sure, however, that moral actions necessarily follow from that knowledge: as Arendt puts it, supported by ample and undeniable empirical evidence, 'moral conduct is not a matter of course'.[1] Aware of this unequal status of knowledge and action, Kant hypothesized that its reason was to be found in the 'sore or foul spot in human nature', which he pinpointed as the 'faculty of lying' (p. 63). He vested his hopes of laying that faculty to rest in another universal human trait, an all-too-human fear of self-contempt, to which the awareness of one's own mendacity would inevitably lead; he was, nevertheless, haunted by the suspicion that this was not a sufficiently strong motive to endow that hope with a guarantee of fulfilment.

All the same, Kant justified his wager on humans' concern for their dignity and self-respect by the ineradicable presence of a 'moral law within me', precisely what 'infinitely raises my worth', through revealing 'a life independent of all animality and even of the whole world of sense' (p. 68). In Arendt's rendition of Kant's reasoning, 'an individual's personal quality is precisely his "moral" quality' (p. 79). Granted that Kant's reasoning was logically impeccable – and so, if tested by the criteria routinely applied to assess the authority of philosophical propositions, the truth of its results would therefore be proved – the thorniest of questions, 'how to persuade the will to accept the dictate of reason' (p. 72), remains, dauntingly, unanswered, alongside its obverse or a corollary, posited already in Plato's parable of the cave: how to 'translate convincingly . . . seen evidence into words and arguments' (p. 88). Hannah Arendt, though, offers an important hint at how to locate the area in which resolution to both haunting queries needs to be sought (though whether it is also to be found there is – as implicitly follows from her argument – a different matter): 'The main distinction, politically speaking, between Thought and Action lies in that I am with my own self or the self of another while I am thinking, whereas I am in the company of the many the moment I start to act' (p. 106). What she implies, I believe, is that, to find the bridge between Thought and Action, one needs to focus on the field occupied and cultivated by sociology (or social psychology) and the art of dialogue.

Scrutinizing that field instead of the field of philosophical thought – notorious for its striving for the logical elegance of a universe freed from its inborn and endemic contradictions – Festinger managed to compose a much more comprehensive map of the manifold roads of escape from the cognitive dissonance arising inside the notoriously confused and confusing gap between moral knowledge and moral conduct. What those varied roads have in common is that they steer clear of ambush by self-contempt – thanks to making the facts of hypocrisy and lying all but invisible, or preventing them from reaching the awareness of the liar. This feat is performed by *faith* – the complete, unshakeable trust and (self-)confidence in something; a firm, indomitable conviction immune to countervailing evidence and argument; firm and indomitable, because it rests on spiritual conviction rather than proof – refuting, in fact, the very need for a proof, and rejecting a priori, or readily dismissing, all evidence casting the belief in doubt as either anomaly or falsehood. The order of logical/empirical reasoning is thereby reversed: as distinct from *knowledge* exposing itself to the critical test of evidence, it is the task of the evidence on offer to prove its accordance with the *faith*. This is the point where Arendt's 'many', our indispensable and inalienable companions from 'the moment I start to act' (and, I'd add, themselves the necessary, *sine qua non* conditions of my starting to act), enter the picture as an irremovable part of the scenery. In the absence of material proof – or if it is refused admission to the court of judgement – my confidence in 'being in the right' and following the correct judgement is supported by Heidegger's 'das Man', Sartre's 'l'on': that means, by my having been attuned to 'what and how this is being done' or rather to 'what (most) people are in the habit of doing'. The more people do it, the safer and more self-confident is the imperturbability of my faith. 'Das Man' and 'l'on' stand for the authority of *numbers*.

Both 'das Man' and 'l'on' have been depicted by their philosopher fathers as more or less timeless features of the human condition: its anthropological – perpetual, perhaps ineffaceable – traits. We need not, however, decide right now whether they are indeed such (namely, eternal and irremovable if tested against the history of *Homo sapiens*) or not, before we observe that, whatever our answer to this question might be, one thing is beyond doubt: some new, *time-bound* circumstances are currently emerging, which set their accompaniment to our actions – their impact and determining role in choosing the targets and the tactics deployed in their pursuit – into the continuing and far from completed process of acquiring new, magnified dimensions and importance. They emerge as the result of several coincidental departures.

One departure is well known to us from our own experience, and that of people around us: we now reside, unprecedentedly, in two different worlds – one 'online', one 'offline' – even if we are apt to switch from one to the other so smoothly that in most cases it is unnoticeable, as there are neither clearly marked borders or immigration booths between them, nor security guards to scrutinize our innocence or immigration officers checking our passports and visas. Quite often we manage to be in both worlds at the same time (think of sitting at the family table or walking in the street, alone or in a group, while exchanging tweets with a Facebook friend hundreds of kilometres away). All the same – knowingly and deliberately, or just matter-of-factly and absent-mindedly – we switch register depending on the momentary drift of our attention: each world has its own set of expectations awaiting those who enter it, and its own patterns of behaviour which they are recommended – and likely – to follow.

A long list of differences between the two worlds can be composed – but one of them seems to weigh most heavily on our responses to the challenges of the 'migration crisis': inside the offline world I am *under control* – expected, and all too often forced, to submit to the control of contingent, capricious circumstances – to obey, to adjust, to negotiate my place, my role as well as the balance of duties and rights – all that guarded and imposed by the explicit or presumed sanction of exclusion and expulsion;

whereas inside the online world I am, on the contrary, in charge and *in control*. Online, I feel I am the manager of circumstances – he who sets the agenda, he who rewards the obedient and punishes the fractious, he who wields the awesome weapon of banishment and exclusion. *I belong* to the offline world – while the online world *belongs to me*. Crossing from the offline to the online world feels like entering a world pliable to my will, ready and keen to comply with my desires.

The advantage of the online alternative over offline existence lies in the promise and expectation of liberation from the discomforts, inconveniences and hardships tormenting the residents of the latter; in a vision of freedom from worry derived not as much from resolving the quandaries and dilemmas that are irresolvable and vexing in the offline part of life as from suspending them, sweeping them under the carpet, removing them from view, and above all making them irrelevant for the task I might have set for myself and intend to pursue. With the annoyances of the world's complexity out of the way, all tasks seem to be so much easier and less strenuous to perform. If their pursuit is found to demand too noxious an effort or proves irritatingly slow in bringing results, they can, effortlessly and with no regret, be abandoned and replaced by others, as yet untried and not discredited, and therefore believed and hoped to be promising; no online choice is ultimate and irreversible, no setback irreparable, no failure irredeemable.

When navigating online, more comfort and less inconvenience may well be chosen as the sole (though dual) compass – to the detriment of all other guides. The more complex, problematic, challenging and straining the tasks we confront offline are, the more seductive the simplifications and facilitations that are often found and always promised in the online alternative become. The offline world is incurably heterogeneous, hetero-nomic and multivocal; it necessitates continuous choosing – hardly any choice being unambiguous and all threatening to stay 'essentially contested', with every one probably carrying consequences eliding even the most painstakingly composed prognoses. By comparison, its online alternative appears enchantingly and cosily straightforward and risk-free, as it offers the chance of reducing complexity and escaping controversy. The more impenetrable the complexity and the less resolvable the controversy, the stronger the temptations of that chance.

The problems generated by the current 'migration crisis', and exacerbated by migration panic, belong to the category of the most complex and controversial: in them, the categorical imperative of morality comes into direct confrontation with the fear of 'the great unknown' epitomized by the masses of strangers at the gate. Impulsive fear aroused by the sight of the aliens bearing inscrutable dangers enters combat with the moral impulse prompted by the sight of human misery. Hardly ever will the challenge to morality as it tries to persuade the will to follow its command be more awesome; and hardly ever will the task of the will as it tries to plug its ears to morality's commands be more excruciating.

All of us might have been cast, at one time or another, simultaneously in the roles of battlefield, soldiers and referees in such a combat. And quite a few of us will therefore be tempted by the 'great simplification' offered by the online shelter. There, inside this shelter, one is saved from the inevitability of confronting the adversary point blank. One may glide over the trap of heart-rending and self-respect-eroding mendacity — by the simple expedient of closing one's eyes to the presence of the adversary and plugging one's ears to his arguments. Both parts of that expedient are easily attainable online, while all but unachievable offline. And so, predictably, many Internet users have been found by researchers to deploy Internet facilities for the purpose of fencing themselves off from the sights and sounds of the battlefield. To the resulting 'comfort zone', only like-minded people are admitted, whereas those on the opposite side of the controversy are barred entry. A modicum of dexterity, determination and consistency in pressing the 'delete' key will suffice to efface the controversy, and its carriers, from sight and memory. Since opening the adopted faith to questioning carries the risk of being proven wrong, and therefore entering a debate feels like an option that is better avoided, getting rid of the need to argue the import and gravity of moral imperatives comes as a welcome relief: turning morally blind and deaf, taking an option free of the risks associated with its alternative, will suffice, thank you.

With their morality blinded and struck deaf, no wonder that 'millions of Americans', as shown in the recent study published in the *Proceedings of the National Academy of Science*, 'believe that their side is basically benevolent while the other side is evil and out to get them'.[2] Donald Trump, by far the most popular of the Republican candidates for the American Presidency, a man with a long and continually lengthening record of the dark rhetoric of racial and religious hatred, 'us vs. them invective and refusal to denounce hate-filled speech for some of his supporters', has been diagnosed by Emma Roller, a *New York Times* opinion editor, as 'the perfect candidate for our viral age'.[3] Why? A psychologist from the University of Hawaii found out that the most eagerly shared viral moments are those that 'come directly from the unconscious' – while 'hate, fear of the other, anger – they come directly from the nonconscious.' Loners in front of a phone, tablet or laptop screen, with only 'viral' others present, seem to put reason together with morality to sleep, letting the normally controlled emotions off the leash.

Obviously, the Internet is not *the cause* of the rising numbers of morally blind and deaf internauts – but it greatly facilitates and beefs up that rise.

When seeking the root cause of the tendency

under discussion, one needs to look beyond the tools, and unfold the motives of the tools' users, as well as digging deeper into the reasons for their inclination to grasp enthusiastically the possibilities those tools offer. For the benefits of the new tools to be keenly embraced and joyfully put to use, there must already have been a still unsatisfied need/desire searching for instruments for its gratification. This need/desire is generated by a new mode of human cohabitation that renders inadequate – or insufficiently efficient – the extant know-how and the habitual conduct patterns it was meant to serve. In turn, the appearance of the new tools assists in lifting that need/desire to the level of an uncontested imperative – through making the until recently dominant life modes look inferior: outdated, uncompetitive and all but redundant.

Taking a leaf from Byung-Chul Han's suggestion,[4] we have already characterized the recently emerged kind of society (still in the process of replacing its predecessor, the 'society of discipline') as one of 'performers' (that is, to deploy Louis Althusser's terms, a society 'interpellating' its members first and foremost in their capacity as 'performers'). Let me add now that, unlike the internauts who can be described as 'loners in constant touch', today's performers perform their performances in constant competition and rivalry with each other. Being cast in the capacity of perfomer is the outcome of individualization: of the progressive erosion of communal bonds, leading to the vulnerability, volatility and eventual dismantling of integrated collectivities, abandoning therefore their individual members to the burdensome duties of self-definition, self-assertion and (total) self-care – relying all along on their own resources, capabilities and industry. In the absence of alternative settings, all those duties need to be performed in the framework of the market. Being a performer therefore equals being involved in the market-centred buying/selling of commodities – and it is their individual performance that the performers must bring to the market for sale, having first made it a sellable commodity: that is, attractive to its potential buyers. To do that, they must out-bid and out-sell the other sellers, whom they cannot but regard as actual or potential competitors in the essentially zero-sum game: because other people around – neighbours, workmates or passers-by – have been destined to participate in the same game, they tend to be spontaneously suspected of being ill-intentioned, malevolent rivals and to continue to be so regarded until proven otherwise. The first reaction to the presence of an-Other tends therefore to be one of vigilance and suspicion – a moment of vague anxiety, of an impulse to search for an anchor, all the more nervously for the menace being under-defined. For the duration, following moral imperatives is suspended. Instead of prompting their awakening, reason advises circumspection: let the sleeping morality lie.

And so we are nowadays residing much of the time in a resurrected Hobbesian world of war of all against all. Perhaps we are not really there – but it feels as if we are. Fear has many eyes, and danger has many entrances. Walls are spattered with holes – as safe as threadbare nets rather than ramparts made of concrete. Life feels, indeed, nasty and brutish – the more nasty and more brutish, the longer it lasts. Facebooked friends are fun for shouting together, but, alas, of little if any use when it comes to doing things together – not to mention in the moments (rare if you are lucky, plentiful if you are not) when it comes to *experimentum crucis*: when, in line with the advice offered by the immortal folk wisdom, they would need to deliver proof of being 'friends indeed' – for instance, in the next round of cuts, outsourcings, contractings out, redundancies. At such instants, you are left to stew in your own juice, and to discover that juice to be in horribly insufficient supply.

It feels like being a victim. Of what? Of circumstances over which you have little, if any, influence – let alone control. We tend to call them 'fate'. But calling them by this name only adds offence to an injury: you are not just a failure, but, to double your humiliation and the self-contempt that follows it, you are in addition a myopic, ignorant, or clumsy and blundering failure – fate has no face, and, more often than not, you try to put a face on it in vain. To avoid this offence and to rescue something of their own dignity and self-respect, victims need to locate, pinpoint and name their victimizers; and the victimizers need to have recognizable faces susceptible to being located, pinpointed and name-attached.

Migrants, and particularly the fresh arrivals among them, meet all those conditions very well indeed. Names (at least a generic name) they have been given already (there are plenty of politicians or journalists around, vying to rule over spirits and thoughts, all too ready and in a hurry to supply them and, as to the job of locating them, to do it, obligingly, for you). And the results are as easy to get to and as trustworthy (indeed, self-evident) as two and two making four: you don't remember knowing that your job was fragile and your well-being volatile before their appearance on the street – while now, once they have arrived or are on their way in, you know only too well that this is the case.

The mechanism for singling out the culprits of victimization appears flawless and unbeatable. It could indeed be so, were it not for the presence of a counterforce: of the phenomenon of encounter, leading to a dialogue that aims if not at an unconditional agreement, then surely at mutual understanding. How can an understanding, defined by Ludwig Wittgenstein in his *Philosophical Investigations* as 'knowing how to go on' (that is: getting rid of, or at least mitigating, uncertainty, that mother of all fears), be achieved? Hans-Georg Gadamer, one of the greatest philosophers of the past century, showed the way in his *Truth and Method*: understanding is a process of 'fusion of horizons'. It consists, as Jeff

Malpas phrased it in his account – in my view, the best available – of the substance of Gadamer's philosophy, in 'establishing a common framework or 'horizon' . . . (*Horizontverschmelzung*)'.[5] Horizons of knowledge, drawn respectively by languages deployed by all parts of humanity meeting and entering in conversation – languages that each of the parts deploy in order, with their help, to grasp, make sense of and accommodate the world they live in (their *Lebenswelte*) – are coming closer to the point of melting and blending. But, let me add, for that to happen, for the two realms of the unfamiliar to become familiar to both sides of the conversation, the two heretofore separate – at odds with each other and for that reason mutually alien – 'lived worlds' need first to come, progressively, closer to overlapping. *Horizontverschmelzung* and *Lebenswelteverschmelzung* intertwine, conditioning each other, steering and seeing through all the way to whatever passes as their successful completion.

Yet we need keep in mind that an undetachable part of Gadamer's conception is recognition of the all-but-defining mark of understanding: that it is a process forever incomplete and *in statu nascendi*, on-going, unended and probably unfinishable. Hence Gadamer's insistence on understanding being 'not reducible to method or technique'. Whatever methods or techniques may happen to be applied in the conversation aimed at understanding, need and tend to emerge – as well as to be renegotiated and revised – in the course of that conversation. This idea was to be developed by Richard Sennett in his postulate that all dialogue should be 'informal' – that is, we should abstain from fixing the procedural rules of conversation ahead of its starting.

To sum up, let me quote from Malpas' analysis once more:

> The basic model of understanding that Gadamer finally arrives at in *Truth and Method* is that of conversation. A conversation involves an exchange between conversational partners that seeks agreement about some matter at issue; consequently, such an exchange is never completely under the control of either conversational partner, but is rather determined by the matter at issue . . . Since both conversation and understanding involve coming to an agreement, so Gadamer argues that all understanding involves something like a

common language, albeit a common language that is itself formed in the process of understanding itself.

In other words, just as the proof of the pudding is in the eating, the proof of the conversation as the royal road to mutual understanding, reciprocated regard and eventually agreement (even if only an agreement reduced to 'agreeing to disagree') is in entering it and conducting it with a view to jointly negotiating the obstacles bound to arise in its course. Whatever the obstacles, and however immense they might seem, conversation will remain *the* royal road to agreement and so to peaceful and mutually beneficial, cooperative and solidary coexistence simply because it has no competitors and so no viable alternative. Let's read attentively, as well as memorize, Appiah's injunction:

The model I'll be returning to [in his study of the impending cosmopolitanization of human residence on Earth] is that of conversation – and, in particular, conversation between people from different ways of life. The world is getting more crowded: in the next half a century the population of our once foraging species will approach nine billion. Depending on the circumstances, conversations across boundaries can be delightful, or just vexing: what they mainly are, though, is inevitable.

Appiah's words sound, uncannily, like a fitting conclusion to what the 'migration crisis' has revealed about the current state of the world we share and the options we all – whether we like it or not – face, and between which we will have, willy-nilly, to choose in the foreseeable future.

Notes

1 Migration Panic and its (Mis)uses

1 See Michel Agier, *Managing the Undesirables*, trans. David Fernbach, Polity, 2011, p. 3.
2 See www.bbc.co.uk/news/uk-31748423.
3 Robert Winder, *Bloody Foreigners: The Story of Immigration to Britain*, Abacus, 2013, p. xiii.
4 See Zygmunt Bauman, *Wasted Lives: Modernity and Its Outcasts*, Polity, 2003.
5 Paul Collier, *Exodus: Immigration and Multiculturalism in the 21st Century*, Oxford University Press, 2013 – here quoted from the 2014 Penguin edition, pp. 50–1.
6 www.theguardian.com/commentisfree/2015/dec/11/the-media-needs-to-tell-the-truth-on-migration-not-peddle-myths.

7 As retold on www.taleswithmorals.com/aesop-fable-the-hares-and-the-frogs.htm.

8 'Marine's prospects for power may be limited, but her appeal is as strong as ever for France's growing numbers of disgruntled and disaffected. That French "ouf" of relief? It's also the noise you make when you get a fist in the abdomen', commented the BBC after the second round of the French 2015 regional elections, from which the ruling Socialist Party candidates had to withdraw to stop the National Front, by the same token paving the way to victory for their main adversary, the right-wing Republicans of M. Sarkozy (www.bbc.co.uk/news/world-europe-35088276). But 'Meanwhile unemployment rises; terror stalks; the grim insurrectionary mood continues to spread.'

9 Jonathan Rutherford, *After Identity*, Laurence and Wishart, 2007, p. 60.

2 Floating Insecurity in Search of an Anchor

1 www.huffingtonpost.com/entry/hollande-attacks-borders-curfew_56467d29e4b045bf3def3699.

2 http://foreignpolicy.com/2015/11/20/hollandes-post-paris-power-grab.

3 http://europe.newsweek.com/after-paris-hollan
  des-popularity-soars-highest-level-three-years-
  400299?rm=eu.

4 http://hungarianspectrum.org/2015/12/18/hun
  garians-fear-of-migrants-and-terrorism.

5 www.nytimes.com/2015/12/31/opinion/americas-
  bountifulchurn.html?emc=edit_th_20151231&nl
  =todaysheadlines&nlid=43773237&_r=0.

6 www.theguardian.com/commentisfree/2015/dec/
  14/europe-refugees-syrians-terror-moas.

7 www.euractiv.com/sections/global-europe/best-
  weapons-against-terrorism-320551.

8 See Erving Goffman, *Stigma: Notes on the
  Management of Spoiled Identity*, Penguin Books,
  1968, particularly ch.1, 'Stigma and Social
  Identity'.

9 www.gettyimages.co.uk/detail/news-photo/dep
  artment-of-homeland-security-chief-jeh-john
  son-speaks-at-news-photo/502828982.

10 www.theguardian.com/world/2015/dec/25/
  david-miliband-interview-syrian-refugees-us-uk.

11 www.euractiv.com/sections/global-europe/best-
  weapons-against-terrorism-320551.

3 On Strongmen's (or Strongwomen's) Trail

1 See www.socialeurope.eu/2015/12/the-revolt-of-the-anxious-class.

2 See http : / / inthesetimes . com / article / 18678 / bringing-socialism-back-how-bernie-sanders-is-reviving-an-american-tradition.

3 Running for the Democratic nomination for the forthcoming presidential election on a 'democratic socialism' ticket. As the *New York Times* reports, 'In an address Thursday afternoon at Georgetown University, Mr. Sanders argued that the redistribution of wealth was at the heart of the American social contract, seeking to link himself with the legacies of the Rev. Dr. Martin Luther King Jr. and Franklin D. Roosevelt. The applause he drew should come as little surprise: Sixty-nine percent of Sanders supporters see socialism in a positive light, versus just 21 percent who view it negatively. Even most of those supporting Hillary Rodham Clinton for the Democratic nomination approve of socialism, 52 percent to 32 percent' (www.nytimes.com/politics/first-draft/2015/11/20/poll-watch-democrats-even-clinton-supporters-warm-to-socialism/?_r=0).

4 Quoted, after Ken Hirschkop, 'Fear and Demo-cracy: an Essay on Bakhtin's Theory of Carnival', *Associations*, 1997, 1, 209–304, from Bakhtin's *Rabelais and His World*, MIT Press, 1968.

5 Zygmunt Bauman, *In Search of Politics*, Polity, 1999, pp. 58–9.

6 Roberto Calasso, *K.*, trans. Geoffrey Brock, Vintage Books, 2006.

7 In *La Société de la fatigue*, Circê, 2014 (German original: *Müdigkeitgesellschaft*, 2010).

8 The full text can be found in *Franz Kafka: The Collected Short Stories*, Penguin Books, 1988, p. 432; also at http://zork.net/~patty/pattyland/kafka/parables/prometheus.htm. Both of these use Willa and Edwin Muir's translation of 1933.

9 *La Fatigue d'être soi*, Odile Jacob, 2008.

10 Han, *La Société de la fatigue*, p. 55.

11 Ivor Southwood, *Non-Stop Inertia*, Zero Books, 2010, pp. 37, 15.

12 Isabell Lorey, *State of Insecurity*, Verso, 2015, p. 2.

13 *Ibid.*, p. 13.

14 Cf. Carl Cederström and André Spiser, *The Wellness Syndrome*, Polity, 2015, p. 6.

15 See Ulrich Beck, *A God of One's Own*, Polity, 2010, p. 62.

16 Ulrich Beck, *Cosmopolitan Vision*, trans. Ciaran Cronin, Polity, 2006.

4 Together and Crowded

1 As quoted in Stéphane Dufoix, *Diasporas*, University of California Press, 2015, p. 35. 'Being sedentary', Dufoix concludes, 'is a recent development in human history' (p. 36).
2 Kevin Kenny, *Diaspora*, Oxford University Press, 2013, p. 17.
3 See Kwame Anthony Appiah, *Cosmopolitanism: Ethics in a World of Strangers*, Penguin, 2007.
4 https://www.mtholyoke.edu/acad/intrel/kant/kant1.htm.
5 Hannah Arendt, 'Some Questions of Moral Philosophy', in Arendt, *Responsibility and Judgment*, Schocken Books, 2003, pp. 50–2.
6 See Leon Festinger, 'Cognitive Dissonance', *Scientific American*, 1962, 207(4), 93–107.
7 http://news.yahoo.com/economic-migrants-children-human-shields-czech-leader-154015439.html.
8 www.theguardian.com/media/greenslade/2015/jul/30/calais-migrants-crisis-national-newspapers-blame-french.

9 www.nytimes.com/2015/12/26/us/thriving-in-tex
as-amid-appeals-to-reject-syrian-refugees.html?
emc=edit_th_20151226&nl=todaysheadlines&n
lid=43773237&_r=0.

10 www.dailymail.co.uk/news/article-3301963/
Katie-Hopkins-not-face-charges-allegations-inci
ted-racial-hatred-article-comparing-migrants-
cockroaches.html.

5 Troublesome, Annoying, Unwanted: Inadmissible

1 'Hungary's Migrant Stance, Once Denounced, Gains Some Acceptance', *New York Times*, 21 December 2015.

2 *Gérer les indésirables*, Flammarion, 2008; here quoted from *Managing the Undesirables*, trans. David Fernbach, Polity, 2011, pp. 4, 3.

3 www.migranttales.net, 21 December 2015.

4 www.theguardian.com/world/2015/dec/22/brit
ain-can-no-longer-sit-out-refugee-crisis-as-eu-
prepares-for-greater-numbers.

5 Paul Collier, 'Beyond the Boat People: Europe's Moral Duty to Refugees', *Social Europe*, 15 July 2015.

6 Anthropological vs Time-bound Roots of Hatred

1 Hannah Arendt, 'Some Questions of Moral Philosophy', in Arendt, *Responsibility and Judgment*, Schocken Books, 2003, p. 62.

2 As reported by Arthur C. Brooks in the *New York Times* on 26 December 2015: http://nytimes.com/2015/12/27/opinion/sunday/the-real-victims-of-victimhood.html?em.

3 www.nytimes.com/2015/12/29/opinion/campaign-stops/donald-trumps-unstoppable-virality.html?emc=edit_ty_20151229&nl=opinion&nlid=43773237.

4 In *La Société de la fatigue*, Circê, 2014 (German original: *Müdigkeitgesellschaft*, 2010).

5 Jeff Malpas, 'Hans-Georg Gadamer', in Edward N. Zalta (ed.), *The Stanford Encyclopedia of Philosophy* (Summer 2015 edition), http://plato.stanford.edu/archives/sum2015/entries/gadamer.